Interviewing

for Child Sexual Abuse:

Strategies

for Balancing Forensic

and

Therapeutic Factors

Melissa McDermott Steinmetz, ACSW

Jalice Publishers

Notre Dame, Indiana

Interviewing for Child Sexual Abuse: Strategies for Balancing Forensic and Therapeutic Factors.

Published by Jalice Publishers, P.O. Box 455, Notre Dame, Indiana 46556. 219-232-9534.

Library of Congress Catalogue Card No. 97-072910

Steinmetz, Melissa McDermott

    Interviewing for Child Sexual Abuse: Strategies for Balancing Forensic and Therapeutic Factors

    1. Child Sexual Abuse – Manuals, Handbooks, etc.   2. Investigations   3. Forensic Interviewing   I. Steinmetz, Melissa McDermott II. Title

    1997   Library of Congress Card Number

    ISBN 0-962737-9-3

Statement of Intention

This book was developed to be a resource to those professionals who investigate allegations of child sexual abuse. It is based on the practices and research present in the field at the time of its publication. By no means does the reading of this book certify an individual to be a forensic interviewer, nor does the author state that the practices described in the book are the final doctrine for investigative interviewing. Rather, the practices are those that have proved in her practice to be forensically and therapeutically sound. The reading of this book should be complemented by professional training, supervision, and an ongoing review of the literature and research.

Acknowledgements

If I had only known what the process of writing a book entailed... I could not have accomplished this task without the support and inspiration of others. It is with sincere gratitude that I would like to express my appreciation to the following:

To my nephew Benjamin, who through his delightful smiles and awe at everything that life has to offer reminded me of the joys of childhood.

To my husband, Bill, who clearly understands the importance my work has for me and thus, so wonderfully encouraged me and tolerated having a part-time wife.

To Tom Balthazor, for his never-ending belief in me, for his ceaseless hours of input on this book and for professionally and personally being available throughout my professional career.

To Kee MacFarlane, Lisa Fey-Williams, Ed Hudson, John Nolan, Connie Carnes, and Betty Brewe, for reviewing and commenting on the manuscript.

To my mother, Gail, and my father, Jim, who provided me with so many wonderful opportunities and a strong foundation.

To Coral Cadman, who indicated that the time was correct for writing this book.

To Rosa Stone, for her enthusiasm, humor, and eternal support.

To Daryl Abbott, who took a risk on me numerous times, and through whose confidence and patience allowed me to grow.

To Cyndy Searfoss, Liz Visser, and Ellen Balthazor for their expertise in editing. And to Dr. Bombay for helping me through the rounds of revisions.

To Jon Conte, for initiating me into the field of child sexual abuse treatment.

To Tom and Ineke for providing me the opportunity to put my thoughts in print.

To Seamus, for keeping me calm throughout my years in this field and during the process of writing this book.

This book is dedicated to the numerous children who through their experiences and struggles have taught and inspired me.

My hope is that their lives will be abundant with joy, a sense of personal completeness, and dignity.

...And for Wilbur and Lula.

TABLE OF CONTENTS

Appendices

Chapter 1

INTRODUCTION

Child sexual abuse is a familiar phenomenon in our culture. During the last three decades, efforts have arisen to combat the problem. In 1963, state legislatures began to enact mandatory reporting laws; now, professionals in every state are mandated to report allegations of alleged abuse (Sheppard & Zangrillo, 1995). These reports are to be received by either child protective services or law enforcement agencies, which are required to notify each other of the allegation.

In the mid-1980s, the concept of a multidisciplinary team for the investigation of child abuse emerged. In 1985, the first Children's Advocacy Center opened in Huntsville, Alabama, and several states were developing and implementing multidisciplinary teams. The rationale of the team approach to child abuse investigations was:

1. The trauma to which the child is subjected (systemic induced abuse) could be minimized by decreasing the number of times and professionals to whom the child needed to make statements;

2. By building a partnership between disciplines, the quality of evidence obtained for civil and criminal proceedings would be enhanced; and

3. Through teamwork, the likelihood of conflict between the investigating agencies would be reduced (National Institute of Justice, 1993 and National Network of Children's Advocacy Centers, 1994).

Notwithstanding the good intentions of this approach, difficulties in the diverse disciplines' ideologies, missions, and strategies have been documented and addressed (Pence & Wilson, 1994). No matter from which discipline a professional response initiates, child abuse investigations are complex. Walsh (1995) presented the following problems typically encountered in child abuse investigations:

1. Because of their limited physical and mental development, children are usually unable to protect themselves.

2. These crimes are usually conducted in one-on-one settings, in a private place.

3. Defendants in child abuse cases usually do not brag about their crimes.

4. Children are often viewed as less credible or competent than the alleged perpetrator.

5. These crimes often have no physical evidence, or if it exists, it does not prove who

the perpetrator was.

6. These crimes involve concurrent civil and criminal investigations.

7. These cases often cross jurisdictional lines.

8. These crimes are frequently investigated by inexperienced or poorly trained personnel.

9. These crimes are usually not isolated incidents. They take place over an extended period of time, involving more than one crime scene.

10. For many reasons, children do not disclose, they partially disclose, or the disclosure is delayed.

11. Children require specially trained interviewers.

12. Children often do not want the offender punished. They just want the abuse to stop.

13. The criminal justice system has many deficits in working with children.

14. Communities are in denial about the problem. People often do not wish to become involved.

Despite these problems, child sexual abuse cases must be investigated. Investigating allegations of child sexual abuse should be a balancing act of the forensic and the therapeutic elements. An investigative interviewer needs to discover the truth; the forensic issue is the facts, just the facts. However, a clinical interviewer must allow the child to have and acknowledge related feelings; the therapeutic issue is the expression of emotions in a nurturing environment. These approaches, forensic and therapeutic, differ in style and traditionally have been thought of as incompatible.

Stereotypically, the therapeutic intervention places the interviewer in the role of an advocate who assumes the child is telling the truth, whereas the customary forensic focus is fact-finding by a neutral interviewer. In forensic inquiries, alternative explanations are explored and obtaining corroborating details is imperative. In therapeutic assessments, subjective interpretations and nonspecific accounts of abuse are sufficient. Finally, in the therapeutic process the credibility of the child is not questioned and the means by which information is obtained is not ordinarily of concern. In a forensic investigation, establishing the child's competency is a concern, and the way information is acquired is strictly governed (Raskin & Esplin, 1991; Sorenson, 1992).

However, an interviewer can be a neutral truth-seeker, who explores all the possible explanations and gathers as many details as possible in a legally sound framework. The forensically and therapeutically balanced interviewer can offer the child support by being present in a nurturing but not leading manner. It is a balancing act that an interviewer needs to master and continually fine-tune.

The role and responsibility of the interviewer is to have a solid knowledge base on issues related to child sexual abuse and investigations. An interviewer should be proficient in research and practice. The interviewer should be knowledgable about suggestibility, memory, styles of questioning, language acquisition, developmental issues, validity of allegations, and competency requirements.

Furthermore, an interviewer needs to be sensitive to the child's needs and the peculiarities of child sexual abuse. The emphasis of investigative interviewing is to minimize the harm to the child while gathering crucial information. It is important to remember that one is working with a child who may have been victimized rather than a victimized child. Two points should be accentuated here. First, the interviewer is responding to an allegation, something that may have happened, rather than something that definitely happened. Second, the interviewer is responding to a child who, if the allegation is substantiated, has victimization as part of his/her makeup; the child is not a victim, which would imply that victimhood is the child's sole identity.

If the child has been victimized, an interviewer should not assume that victimization equals traumatization. There is not a set response pattern to sexual abuse. Summitt (1983) introduced the child sexual abuse accommodation syndrome. The syndrome, which is not a diagnosis, has five characteristics that demonstrate the logical pattern and sequence of interaction among the child, the perpetrator, and potential caregivers (Summitt, 1994). The syndrome explains the ways in which secrecy is upheld in the abusive relationship and how a child feels helpless and entrapped, thus accommodating the abuse and survival strategies in order to survive. Finally, it explains the likelihood for delayed, conflictual, and unconvincing disclosure and retraction. This syndrome does not imply that every child will exhibit every characteristic. Children and their responses vary, based on the situations, available resources, and their ego strength.

Interviewers should be aware that they are the gatekeepers to the child's recovery. The investigative process, including the interview, is the gateway. The child and family members cannot begin to productively address child sexual abuse and its consequences in a direct manner until disclosure has occurred and the abuse has ended. How the interviewer addresses the child can significantly affect the child's disclosure and perception of the system.

Respect for the child is essential to the interview process. Disclosure is a process (Sorenson & Snow, 1991). It is unrealistic to expect a child to develop trust immediately with an unfamiliar interviewer and to share the details of sexual victimization. Some children will need a number of interviews. Other children may never disclose their victimization. It is important not to push or pressure a reluctant child into a disclosure. Rather, professionals should gather evidence elsewhere, and if necessary attempt another interview with the child. Finally, it should be remembered that if a child has been victimized and discloses the victimization, he/she is effectively handing his/her life to the interviewer on a silver platter. It is important to respect the gift given you and to respect the giver.

The need for a balanced forensic and therapeutic approach is as much for the benefit of the child as it is for the multidisciplinary team. By using this approach, the child protective services worker can identify the need for protection of the child and his/her siblings; when applicable, treatment providers can begin to identify the impact of the abuse; and law enforcement/prosecution officials can determine the likelihood that a crime was committed. All aspects of the case carry the same weight and importance.

Much of the labor related to investigative interviewing occurs before the face-to-face encounter with the child. Preparation is vital to a comprehensive investigation. It is as essential as the actual dialogue with the child. When meticulously performed, the work results in a balanced and sound investigation. This book's organization reflects this need. Chapters 2, 3, 4, and 5 focus on the interviewer's knowledge base. Chapters 6 and 7 address the interviewer's characteristics and the physical environment in which the interview should be conducted. Chapters 8 through 12 take the reader through the interview process. Chapter 13 concentrates on cases in which an extended evaluation is necessary, followed by a chapter on the nonoffending parent and the conclusion.

Although a significant problem, interviewing developmentally and physically disabled children will not be addressed in this book. This is not to minimize the prevalence of abuse in this population. Research estimates that disabled children are abused at four to ten times the rate of nondisabled children (Baladerian, undated). Although some strategies remain the same, the communication styles and methods needed in these interviews are different. Special training, beyond the scope of this book, is required for investigative interviewing with this population.

Investigative interviewing is the combination of a secure knowledge base and the acquisition and refinement of critical interviewing skills. This combination facilitates a forensically and therapeutically sound investigative interview. With this balance in an interviewer's repertoire, there is a greater likelihood that the truth can be discovered in the majority of child sexual abuse allegations.

REFERENCES

Baladerian, N. (Undated). *Disability, Abuse, and Personal Rights.* A project of SPECTRUM Institute. Culver City, CA: SPECTRUM Institute.

National Network of Children's Advocacy Centers (1994). *Best practices: A guidebook to establishing a children's advocacy center program.* Huntsville, AL: National Network of Children's Advocacy Centers.

National Institute of Justice, Office of Victims of Crime, Office of Juvenile Justice and Delinquency Prevention and the National Center on Child Abuse and Neglect. (1993). *Joint investigations of child abuse: A report of a symposium.* Washington, DC: National Institute of Justice.

Pence, D., & Wilson, C. (1994). *Team investigation of child sexual abuse: Uneasy alliance.* Thousand Oaks, CA: Sage Publications.

Raskin, D., & Esplin, P. (1991). Statement validity assessment: Interview procedures and content analysis of children's statement of sexual abuse. *Behavioral Assessment, 13,* 265-291.

Sheppard, D., & Zangrillo, P. (1995). *A study to improve law enforcement/child protective services investigations of reported child maltreatment. Final Report.* Washington, DC: Police Foundation and American Public Welfare Association.

Sorenson, T., and Snow, B. (1991). How children tell: The process of disclosure in child sexual abuse. *Child Welfare, 70,* 3-15.

Sorenson, E. (1992). (Untitled). Lecture, National Network of Children's Advocacy Center's Spring Training. Huntsville, AL.

Summitt, R. (1983). The child sexual abuse accommodation syndrome. *Child Abuse and Neglect, 7,* 177-192.

Summitt, R. (1994). Abuse of the child sexual abuse accommodation syndrome. *Journal of Child Sexual Abuse, 1,* 153-164.

Walsh, B. (1995). Plenary Session with M. Steinmetz. *Multi-disciplinary approach: Building a mutually supported collaboration.* Multi-Disciplinary Team Conference. Bozeman, MT.

Chapter 2

MEMORY and SUGGESTIBILITY

Volumes have been written about memory and its relationship with traumatic events. An effective interviewer should have a solid knowledge base regarding trauma and its influence on memory, children's memory capacity, aids to facilitate recall, and suggestibility.

Memory is the process of encoding, storing, and retrieving (Kail, 1990). This is a skill that improves with age (Batterman-Faunce & Goodman, 1993). Orstein (1995) and Orstein, Larus, and Clubb (1991) postulate four theories regarding memory. First, memory of an event can change because of suggestions from others regarding the event, lack of re-instatement, and passage of time. The next theory is that prior knowledge and experience affect what information is stored. With pre-existing knowledge of a similar event, the child is more likely to make sense of the new experience, thus it is easier for the event to be placed in the memory. The third theory relates to the strength of events that are remembered. The strength of the memory is based on such factors as amount of exposure and the age of the child. The last theory is that not everything in memory can be retrieved all of the time, and not everything that is retrieved is reported.

Ordinary memory and traumatic memory differ (Whitfield, 1995). In situations where post-traumatic stress disorder is present memory difficulties may arise (van der Kolk & van der Hart, 1991; van der Kolk & van der Hart, 1994; van der Kolk & Fisler, 1995; and Terr, 1994). The "forgetting" occurs because of the individual's pattern of coping. To avoid the psychological and emotional pain of the trauma, the individual may dissociate, partially repress, or deny the event(s). However, van der Kolk et al. (1991), reports that although the memories are not consciously present, they do remain in the unconscious.

Goodman and Reed (1986) and Goodman, Bottoms, Schwartz-Kenney, and Rudy, (1991) found a relationship between a disturbing event, comprehensive recall, and a decrease in being influenced by suggestible questions. Furthermore, Christianson (1992) reported that core features of emotionally charged events are incorporated into one's memory. Merritt, Orstein, and Spicker (1994) found impressive recall in young children involved in invasive medical procedures. This research found a correlation between stress and subsequent memory. However, Pynoos and Eth (1984) and Terr (1991) found that stressful events are associated with strong memories, but the memories can be inaccurate because of emotional forces.

Research (Fivush & Schwarzmueller, 1995; Fivush & Shukat 1995; Saywitz & Goodman, 1996, and Levine, Saywitz, & Koocher, 1995) has found that children, even preschoolers, are able to recall information effectively. Children have good memory capacity and recall; even 2 to 3 year-olds can describe core features accurately. Although young children can provide accurate accounts, the accounts tend to be briefer. There is a correlation between increased age and the amount of information reported (Goodman & Reed, 1986; Oates & Shrimpton, 1991; Fivush & Schwarzmueller, 1995). Lamb, Sternberg & Esplin, (1995) states that grounds for this tendency is that children's memories may be poorer, their experiences have been limited, thus they do not have a pool of resources from which to draw comparisons. Children do not have extensive vocabulary skills with which to articulate the events.

Dent and Stephenson (1979) submit that free recall is the most accurate form of reporting one's memory. However, Saywitz & Goodman (1996) and Pipe, Gee & Wilson (1993) found that younger children are not as dependable as older children in responding to open-ended questions. Free recall does not yield an abundance of information from these children. Younger children need cues and props to trigger the retrieval and subsequent relaying of memory. Saywitz, Snyder, & Lamphear (1996) found that children produce more elaborate disclosures without the use of leading questions when cue cards assist their memory retrieval. A child needs to be interviewed in a nonintimidating environment (Goodman et al, 1991) with an unbiased interviewer who will use nonsuggestive techniques to jog the child's memory (see Chapter 11 for more detailed information).

Children have a greater ability to remember events in which they participated than those they have observed (Baker-Ward, Hess, & Flannagan, 1990; Tobey & Goodman, 1992). They will have more accurate memories of central/core details. Even as a participant, children will make more errors of omission than commission: They have more of a tendency to leave out details than to create false information (Oates & Shrimpton, 1991; Steward, 1993).

Key to having a child reveal what he/she remembers is motivation. Young children need to be motivated to share their memories (Saywitz, 1994). Lamb, et al. (1995), relates that children are not accustomed to being "informants." They need to know that the interviewer values what they have to say.

Goodman, Rudy, Bottoms, & Aman, (1990) found that a child's willingness to divulge does not necessarily increase with age. Rather, it seems the trend is reversed. Because of motivational factors, such as embarrassment and concern for potential ramifications, children may not disclose details they do remember.

A contentious area, one in which much research and controversy has arisen, is suggestibility. Saywitz and Goodman (1996), report that the ability to resist suggestible influences varies in every age range. Loftus and Wells (1984) and Loftus (1994) state that adults can change their reports after misleading and suggestive questions. Immunity to suggestibility depends on the circumstances and the personality of the individual. However, it has been found (Goodman & Aman, 1991; Ceci & Bruck, 1993; Ceci, Ross, & Toglia, 1987) that younger children can be more suggestible than older ones. Numerous studies have found that younger children are more swayed by leading questions when various factors including repeated questioning are present.

Dent (1990) and Fivush and Schwarzmueller (1995) found that children are more likely to change their accounts when asked for additional details. Ceci and Bruck (1993), propose that repeated questions in an interview relay to a child that his/her first answer was unacceptable. Furthermore, they postulate that repeated questions reveal the interviewer's bias. Subsequently, the child will change his/her answers to please the interviewer. They also found that "supportive statements," such as, "We know something happened," or, "You'll feel better once you tell," again display the interviewer's bias. Thus, there is a greater motivation for the child to fabricate. They further propose that with repeated questions, an "avenue for introjection of misinformation" is provided. However, Goodman et al. (1991), found that repeated misleading questioning regarding possible abusive acts did not necessarily increase the inaccuracies of the child's accounts.

Multiple interviews, which occur over an extended period of time, may affect suggestibility. Ceci and Bruck (1995) propose that the more time between the event and interviews, the greater the chance of memory intrusion by outside sources. They report that there is a greater likelihood that misinformation will be incorporated in the child's report. However, Fivush (1993) and Fivush and Schwarzmueller (1995) relay that multiple interviews do assist recall; additional details are shared in subsequent interviews. They report that inaccuracies and errors do not appear to increase with elapsed time or the number of interviews.

When children are asked to relay information regarding events of which they are uncertain or have incomplete memory, suggestibility may be an influential factor (Goodman, Bottoms, Herscovici, & Shaver, 1989). Children will attempt to answer an adult's question (Ceci & Bruck, 1993). Vrig (1996) found a decrease in changes and inaccurate information if the interviewer allowed the child to respond with "I don't know." Children are more likely to guess, especially if "I don't know" is not presented as an option (Saywitz & Moan-Hardie, 1994).

The environment or interviewer can influence a child's level of suggestibility. If either is intimidating, the child's suggestibility may increase. An intimidating or aggressive interviewer may result in the child becoming avoidant, providing less information, or agreeing to misleading statements. (Goodman et al., 1989; Goodman et al., 1991). Furthermore, if the interviewer is biased and presents information in an accusatory manner, Tobey & Goodman (1992) found inaccuracies occur in preschoolers free recall and spontaneous statements. Ceci, Caves, and Howe, (1981), found that children are sensitive to authority figures and will comply with their agendas.

Suggestibility increases when a child is instilled with a negative stereotype or has negative expectations of an individual (Leichtman & Ceci, 1995). Furthermore, children are more likely to be misled when they do not know what is expected of them (Reed, 1996; and Saywitz & Nathanson, 1992).

Finally, children are more suggestible when they believe that the interviewer is knowledgeable about the allegation. In everyday situations, children are repeatedly shown and told that adults know the answers to the questions they pose, i.e., the teacher who asks the child to respond to a history question. A question that contains information true to the allegation, whether it is a focused or leading question, can imply prior knowledge, thus increasing the child's level of suggestibility (Saywitz, Goodman, Nicholas, & Moan, 1991).

Although the above cited research is based on laboratory studies and not field studies, it does provide an interviewer with invaluable information. First and foremost, the interviewer needs to enter the interview with an open mind. He/she should not have a bias nor look exclusively for confirmatory information. The interviewer should let the child know that he/she is uninformed. Interviewers will need to ask repeated questions, but they should change the phrasing so the child knows that the original response was not inaccurate. Rather, the interviewer is trying to gather all the information. Likewise, an interviewer should focus on asking questions that do not interject new and misleading information. The interviewer needs to emphasize the need for truth, but balance it with permitting the child to answer questions with an "I don't know," "I don't remember," or "I don't understand." To reduce guessing, an interviewer should empower the child to claim a lack of knowledge.

An interviewer needs to look at ways in which he/she can facilitate a child's memory retrieval and its subsequent disclosure without being suggestive. This is achieved through interviewer's questioning styles and presence. Paramount to a child being able to accurately retrieve and report the details of the alleged abuse is for an interviewer to be unbiased and to possess the skills that will enhance the child's delivering of his/her account(s).

REFERENCES:

Baker-Ward, L, Hess, T.M., & Flannagan, D.A. (1990). The effects of involvement on children's memory of events. *Cognitive Development, 5,* 55-69.

Batterman-Faunce, J., & Goodman, G. (1993). *Effects of context on the accuracy and suggestibility of child witnesses.* In G. Goodman and B. Bottoms (Eds.), Child victims, child witnesses (pp. 301-330). NY: Guilford Press.

Ceci, S., Caves, R., & Howe, M. (1981). Children's long term memory for information congruent with their knowledge. *British Journal of Psychology, 72,* 443-450.

Ceci, S., & Bruck, M. (1993). Suggestibility of child witnesses: A historical review and synthesis. *Psychological Bulletin, 113,* 403-439.

Ceci, S., & Bruck, M. (1995). *Jeopardy in the courtroom: A scientific analysis of children's testimony.* Washington, DC: American Psychological Association.

Ceci, S., Ross, D., & Toglia, M. (1987). Age differences in suggestibility: Narrowing the uncertainties. In S.J.Ceci, M.P. Toglia, & D.R. Ross (Eds.), *Children's Eyewitness Memory,* (pp. 79-91). NY: Springer Verlag.

Christianson, S. (1992). Emotional stress and eye witness memory: A critical review. *Psychological Bulletin, 12,* 284-309.

Dent, H. (1990). Interviewing. In J. Doris (Ed.), *Suggestibility in children's recollections,* (pp. 138-146). Washington, DC: American Psychological Association.

Dent, H., & Stephenson, G. (1979). An experimental study of the effectiveness of different techniques of questioning child witnesses. *British Journal of Social and Clinical Psychology, 18,* 41-51.

Fivush, R., & Schwarzmueller, A. (1995). Say it once again: Effects of repeated questions on children's event recall. *Journal of Traumatic Stress, 8,* 555-580.

Fivush, R., & Shukat, J. (1995). Content, consistency, and coherence in early autobiographical memory. In M. Zaragozza, J.R. Graham, G. Hall, R. Hirshman, & Y. Ben-Porath (Eds.), *Memory and testimony in the child witness* (pp. 5-23). Thousand Oaks, CA: Sage Publications.

Fivush, R., (1993). Developmental perspectives on autobiographical recall. In G. Goodman & B. Bottoms (Eds.), *Child victims, child witnesses* (pp. 1-24). New York: Guilford Press.

Goodman, G., Rudy L., Bottoms, B., & Aman, C. (1990). Children's concerns and memories: Issues of ecological validity on the study of children's eyewitness testimony. In R. Fivush and J. Hudson (Eds.), *Knowing and remembering in young children* (pp. 249-284). NY: Cambridge University Press.

Goodman, G., Bottoms, B., Schwartz-Kenney, B., & Rudy, L. (1991). Children's testimony about a stressful event: Improving children's reports. *Journal of Narrative and Life History, 1,* 69-99.

Goodman, G., Bottoms, B., Herscovici, B., & Shaver, P. (1989). Detriments of the child victim's perceived credibility. In S. Ceci, D. Ross, M. Toglia (Eds.), *Perspectives on children's testimony* (pp. 1-22). New York: Springer-Verlog.

Goodman, G., & Aman, C. (1991). Children's use of anatomically detailed dolls to recount an event. *Child Development, 61,* 1859-1871.

Goodman, G., & Reed, R. (1986). Age differences in eyewitness testimony. *Law and Human Behavior, 10,* 317-322.

Kail, R. (1990). *The development of memory in children* (3rd ed.). New York: W.H. Freeman.

Lamb, M., Sternberg, K., & Esplin, P. (1995). Making children into competent witnesses: Reactions to the amicus brief. In re *Michael's Psychology, Public Policy, and Law, 1,* 438-449.

Leichtman, M., & Ceci, S. (1995). Effects of stereotypes and suggestions on preschoolers' reports. *Developmental Psychology, 31,* 568-578.

Levine, M., Saywitz, K., & Koocher, G. (1995). Empirical research on child maltreatment and the law. *Journal of Clinical Child Psychology, 47,* 59.

Loftus, E., & Wells, G. (1984). *Eyewitness testimony: Psychological perspectives.* New York: Cambridge University Press.

Loftus, E. (1994). *The myth of repressed memory: False memories and allegations of sexual abuse.* New York: St. Martin's Press.

Merritt, K., Orstein, P., & Spicker, B. (1994). Children's memory for salient medical procedure: Implications for testimony. *Pediatrics, 94,* 17-23.

Oates, K., & Shrimpton, S. (1991). Children's memory for non-stressful events. *Medical Science and the Law, 31,* 4-10.

Orstein, P. (1995). Children's long term retention of salient personal experiences. *Journal of Traumatic Stress, 8,* 581-605.

Orstein, P., Larus, D., & Clubb, P. (1991). Understanding children's testimony: Implications of research in the development of memory. In R. Vasta (Ed.), *Annals of Child Development* (pp. 145-176). London: Jessica Kingsley Press.

Pipe, M., Gee, S., & Wilson, C. (1993). Cues, props, and context: Do they facilitate children's reports. In G. Goodman, & B. Bottoms (Eds.), *Child victims, child witnesses* (pp. 25-45). NY: Guilford Press.

Pynoos, R., & Eth, S. (1984). The child as witness to homicide. *Journal of Social Issues, 40,* 87-108.

Reed, L.D. (1996). Findings from research on children's suggestibility and implications for conducting child interviews. *Child Maltreatment, 1,* 105-120.

Saywitz, K., Goodman, G., Nicholas, E., & Moan, S. (1991). Children's memories of physical examinations involving genital touch: Implications for reports of child sexual abuse. *Journal of Consulting and Clinical Psychology, 59,* 682-691.

Saywitz, K., & Moan-Hardie, S. (1994). Reducing the potential for distortion of childhood memories. *Consciousness and Cognition, 3,* 408-425.

Saywitz, K., & Nathanson, R. (1992). Effects of environment on children's testimony and perceived stress. In L.D. Reed Findings from research on children's suggestibility and implications for conducting child interviews. *Child Maltreatment, 1*(2), 105-120.

Saywitz, K. (1994). Questioning child witnesses. *Violence Update, 4,* 3-10.

Saywitz, K., & Goodman G. (1996). Interviewing children in and out of court: Current research and practice implications. In J. Briere, L. Berliner, J. Bulkley, C. Jenny, & T. Reid (Eds.), *The APSAC Handbook on Child Maltreatment* (pp. 297-318). Thousand Oaks, CA: Sage Publications.

Saywitz, K., Snyder, L., & Lamphear, V. (1996). Helping children tell what happened: A follow up study of the narrative elaboration procedure. *Child Maltreatment, 1,* 200-212.

Steward, M. (1993). Understanding children's memories of medical procedures: "He didn't touch me and it didn't hurt!" In C.A. Nelson (Ed.), *Memory and Affect in Development* (pp. 171-225). Englewood Cliffs, NJ: Lawrence Erlbaum Associates.

Terr, L. (1991). Childhood traumas: An outline and overview. *American Journal of Psychiatry, 148,* 10-20.

Terr, L. (1994). *Unchained memories: True stories of traumatic memories, Lost and found.* New York: Basic Books.

Tobey, A., & Goodman, G. (1992). Children's eyewitness memory: Effects of participation and forensic context. *Child Abuse and Neglect, 16,* 779-796.

van der Kolk, B., & van der Hart, O. (1991). The intrusive past: The flexibility of memory and the engraving of trauma. *American Imago, 48,* 425-454.

van der Kolk, B., & van der Hart, O. (1994). The body keeps the score: Memory and the evolving psychobiology of posttraumatic stress. *Harvard Review of Psychology, 1,* 253-265.

van der Kolk, B., & Fisler, R. (1995). Dissociation and the fragmentary nature of traumatic memories: Overview and exploratory study. *Journal of Traumatic Stress, 8,* 505-526.

Vrig, A. (1996). Does an explanation of conversation rules reduce suggestibility in child witnesses? In A. Warren, C. Woodall, J. Hunt, & N. Perry. It sounds good in theory but ... Do investigative interviews follow guidelines based on memory research? *Child Maltreatment, 1,* 231-245.

Whitfield, C. (1995). *Memory and abuse: Remembering and healing the effects of trauma.* Deerfield Beach, FL: Health Communications.

Chapter 3

DECREASING THE DIFFERENCE BETWEEN THE INTERVIEWER AND THE CHILD

There is a fundamental impediment to the interviewing process, that of perceived authority. An interviewer needs to be aware of the inherent power he/she possesses. Children have been taught that adults are in charge; adults are in control. Whether a child has been abused by an adult, adolescent or another child, or has not experienced abuse, he/she has been taught to listen to and respect adults. Anything the interviewer can do to diminish this power differential is advantageous to the relationship.

One strategy is for the interviewer to position his/her body below or at the child's eye level. This should be implemented throughout the interview. Upon greeting the child it is recommended that the interviewer immediately bend at the knees and squat to the child's level. This position is more favorable than bending at the waist. The latter can be associated with a massive figure that towers over the child and then descends to possibly admonish or engulf the child. After entering the interview room, the interviewer should place him/herself in a position at or below the child's eye level. This will frequently result in the interviewer being seated on the floor.

Further compounding the power issue is the fact that in some aspects, the interviewer/child relationship mimics the perpetrator/child relationship. Power/control and secrecy are two prominent elements of the abuse relationship. The interviewer is an adult, which implies power, and the child is interviewed in an environment over which the interviewer has control and familiarity. Furthermore, the interview is a situation where typically one adult and one child are alone while discussing secrets.

Another aspect that accentuates the difference between the child and the interviewer is that of knowledge. Again, children have been taught that adults possess more knowlegde than they do. Children are used to seeking out adults for advice and counsel. One way to ease this power differential is to allow the child to guide the interviewer in limited areas of the interview process. During the start of the interview, while rapport is being established, an interviewer can simply ask the child for direction. Simple questions such as, "Where should I sit?" "Is it okay for me to sit here?" or, "What should I know about you?" can greatly assist a child in feeling empowered.

Furthermore, an interviewer could act forgetful and confused (Hindman, 1987). This not only helps to equalize the relationship between the interviewer and the child, but it also allows the interviewer to demonstrate to the child that "I don't know" is an acceptable answer. This will be discussed further in Chapter 10. Being forgetful and asking for a restatement provides the interviewer with the opportunity to repeat questions without giving the child the impression that his/her answer was not correct.

A final area regarding knowledge and its impact on highlighting the disparity of the relationship is language. It can appear as though the interviewer is speaking a foreign language to the child if the sentence structure and word application are incongruent with the child's development. This will be discussed in detail in Chapter 4.

An interviewer must be aware of childhood developmental issues and their impact on sexual abuse allegations. Each child has his/her own way of relating to the world, based on age. It is important for an interviewer to know the developmental stages of childhood. An interviewer can sabotage the interview if he/she expects more or less than a child can provide. An interviewer should review what is appropriate for an age range prior to an interview. This is done by reviewing common developmental charts that state what social, emotional, cognitive, and physical abilities can be expected of a child in a specific age group. It is important for the interviewer to remember that chronological age is not always synonymous with developmental age. However, a review of a developmental chart provides the interviewer with a starting point from which he/she can assess the child during the rapport building phase of the interview. This will be discussed further in Chapter 10.

An interviewer should also be aware of issues associated with disclosure for each age group. No matter what the child's age range, it is important for the interviewer to take time prior to the interview to reflect on the child's possible reasons for disclosing and not disclosing. What are the motivating factors for this child? Children in sexual abuse recovery treatment have informed us that disclosure is one of the most difficult parts of the process. Several children and adolescents have said it was easier living with the abuse than disclosing it. At least for a child, the abuse and the abusive environment are a known commodity, whereas the system and its response are unknown and quite frightening.

The interviewer should be aware of the context of the child's initial disclosure. Was it direct, the child stating, "_____ is touching me"? Was it indirect, the child reporting clues, "_____ wouldn't let me sleep last night," or, "_____ has funny underwear"? Was it a third-person disclosure, "What would you do if you knew a little boy was being touched?" Or was it a disclosure with strings attached, "I have something inportant to tell you, but you have to promise not to tell anyone"? These types of disclosures usually make the interview easier because the child has mentally prepared for the disclosure. The child has weighed the pros and cons of telling and has chosen to directly or indirectly disclose. However, if the disclosure is of an accidental nature, one that occurred as the result of emotional upheaval or a referral based on observed behaviors, the interview may be more difficult. In accidental disclosures, the child is less prepared to deal with the implications.

Regardless of the type of disclosure, there are issues that each age group presents. Although not found in every child, they are frequently displayed. It is important for an interviewer to be familiar with them.

Preschool-age children are often the most difficult to interview. Their speech and language skills can be minimal and typically their attention spans are limited. As a result, the interviewer needs to perform a more directed interview. Often with children in this age range, very direct or focused questions need to be asked (Toth, 1995). Young children do not monitor their language for errors, omissions, and inconsistencies. They will unknowingly mistake the identity and meaning of words (Steward, Bussey, Goodman, & Saywitz, 1993). Preschoolers have a difficult time freely talking about situations. Interviews are typically shorter and more focused with this age group. These children will usually be able to provide the who, what, and where of the allegation. As such, investigators will need to rely on collateral sources to corroborate the child's story. This is true for all reports, however, with younger children it is especially true. Furthermore, sequencing in relaying the details of a situation is difficult (Steward, et al., 1993). It is advantageous to have visual cues to assist them. For example, when discussing the alleged abuse the anatomically detailed dolls or charts could be used.

Children are regularly socialized through rewards and punishment; thus if the alleged perpetrator used threats or bribery, disclosure may be extremely difficult with preschoolers. Core issues (Erikson, 1963) for this age group are autonomy versus shame and doubt (18 months to 3 years) and initiative versus guilt (3 to 6 years.) This correlates with gaining control and becoming purposeful, both of which are discouraged in an abusive environment.

Children ages 5 to 12 years offer a unique set of issues. Their critical developmental task is industry/competence versus inferiority (Erikson, 1963). Being sexually victimized and placed in a position of potential disclosure further exaggerates the challenge of this task. Children in this age range typically know why they are being interviewed, and especially older children know the consequences of disclosing. Children in this age bracket are still connected to their families. Younger ones usually see their parents as always being correct. The disclosure process is impeded if an interviewer looks at and describes abuse only as bad actions versus good actions. However, because this age range sees the world primarily in black and white, it can be beneficial to stress the importance of telling the truth.

Older children in this age range frequently have grave concerns about being removed from their families. For these children, the playground and the neighborhood are the primary arenas in which they learn. They may have heard and seen what happened to other children reporting abuse, and assumed that their fate will be the same.

A recurrent interview question posed by this population, no matter whether the alleged abuser is a nuclear family member, is, "Are you going to take me away from my home?" It is important for an interviewer to not directly answer this question, because the interviewer does not know if there is an abuser, if so, who it is, and what protective efforts will be needed. Rather, as a rule of thumb on highly charged questions such as these, the interviewer should respond, "I don't know. How come you are concerned about that? What makes you think that you might be removed from your home?"

If abuse has occurred, children between 5 and 12 are aware of the consequences of disclosure and because the family is pivotal in their existence, these children may have a greater likelihood of recanting. For any age range, though, the interviewer and the multidisciplinary team need to be aware of the potential for recantation. As such, specific support needs to be made to the child and family and responsibility needs to be placed with, and preferably assumed by, the perpetrator to reduce the potential for retraction (Summitt, 1983).

Adolescents, meanwhile, are focused on their identity and the development of values; foremost for this group is the question, "Who am I?" If the child has been abused, the answer to the question can be extremely skewed. This is an age group with which the interviewer easily can be caught off guard. The false assumption that older children will be easier to interview can be dangerous. On the contrary, adolescents can be extremely difficult to engage in the interview. They frequently question authority figures and believe that adults can't understand what they are going through, let alone be able to talk with them. Furthermore, for protection adolescents may assume a "macho" or defensive stance. It is important for an interviewer to recognize that they are still children.

Adolescents often equate blame with responsibility. For all age groups, the interview process places the child in an apparent omnipotent predicament: The child believes that by disclosing, he/she is the one who will determine whether the abuse will end, and whether the perpetrator will be punished. Realistically, it is the perpetrator's actions that lead to law enforcement involvement; it is the prosecutor's office that determines whether charges will be filed; it is a twelve-person jury that may ultimately weigh the evidence; and it is the judge who will impose the sentence. However, to the disclosing child, his/her belief is it is he/she who causes everything to happen.

Moreover adolescents have additional beliefs concerning responsibility and blame and frequently are unable to differentiate between these concepts. The interview environment is not the proper place to deliberate the meanings of these words. Rather, this should be a treatment issue. In situations such as acquaintance rape, the adolescent often feels responsible because he/she was involved in such high-risk behaviors as violating a curfew, consuming alcohol and/or drugs, or engaging in a loosely defined social relationship.

For adolescent incest victims, disclosure may end long-term abuse. Members of this group may feel responsible for not reporting sooner or for reaping physical or material benefits from the abuse. Further compounding these cases is the child's perceived responsibility for ending the relationship. This frequently involves grief and loss.

Interviewers must also be cognizant of the reality that victimized children can become victimizers (Ryan, 1989; Cunningham & MacFarlane 1991; Gil & Cavanaugh Johnson, 1993; and Way & Balthazor, 1990). There is a great likelihood that an interviewer will see many children, and based on percentages many more adolescents, who transitioned from victim to victimizer. An interviewer should always be careful not to judge an alleged perpetrator as good or bad. To do so could cause the child to withhold information.

Finally, of all the age groups, this is the one in which the interviewer's gender may have the greatest impact. For all children, the gender of the interviewer should be based on the child's personality and the alleged abuser's profile. However, with pre-adolescents and adolescents, discussing matters related to sexuality either can be extremely embarrassing or seductive.

Interviewers can decrease the power difference in the interview setting. By taking the necessary steps before and during the interview, interviewers can greatly enhance the likelihood that productive information will be exchanged.

REFERENCES:

Cunningham, C., & MacFarlane, K. (1991). *When children molest children: Group treatment strategies for young sexual abusers.* Orwell, VT: Safer Society Press.

Erikson, E.H. (1963). *Childhood and society.* New York: Norton.

Gil, E., & Cavanaugh-Johnson, T. (1993). *Sexualized children: Assessment and treatment of sexualized children and children who molest.* Rockville, MD: Launch Press.

Hindman, J. (1987). *Step by step: Sixteen steps toward legally sound sexual abuse investigations.* Ontario, OR: Alexandria Press.

Ryan, G. (1989). Victim to victimizer: Rethinking victim treatment. *Journal of Interpersonal Violence, 4,* 325-341.

Steward, M., Bussey, K., Goodman, G., & Saywitz, K. (1993). Implications of developmental research for interviewing children. *Child Abuse and Neglect, 17,* 25-37.

Summitt, R. (1983). The child sexual abuse accommodation syndrome. *Child Abuse and Neglect, 7,* 177-192.

Toth, P. (1995). Dialogue from author's presentation: Interviewing sexually abused children. Huntsville, AL: Office of Victims of Crime Federal Training Day. .

Way, I., & Balthazor, T. (1990). *A manual for structured group treatment with adolescent sexual offenders.* Notre Dame, IN: Jalice Publishers.

Chapter 4

LANGUAGE AND QUESTIONING

"Children of all ages can tell us what they know if we ask them the right question in the right way" (Walker, 1994). Asking the right question in the right way not only means asking a developmentally appropriate question, but also asking a forensically and therapeutically appropriate question. An interviewer can miss gathering the details of an event if the question is not age appropriate. A child can become reluctant to share the details if the question is not presented therapeutically. Also, an interviewer can contaminate or destroy an entire criminal case if the questions are not asked in a forensically sound manner.

Questioning styles have been the center of much media attention and many professional debates. Ceci and Bruck (1995) discuss a dichotomy of aggressive or passive interviewing practices. Other professionals and researchers (Faller, 1990; Lamb, Sternberg & Esplin, 1995; Myers, 1992; and Boat and Everson, 1986) advocate a continuum of open-ended to closed-ended questions. Although their terminologies vary, these professionals propose a funnel style of questioning. An interviewer should begin with open-ended questions, "Do you know why you are here today?" followed by focused questions that ask about people, feelings, and touching. Following the open-ended questions, multiple choice and yes-no questions can be utilized. However, with these last two types of questions the interviewer needs to be aware that he/she will receive fewer details from the child. Finally, if necessary, the interviewer may need to resort to direct questions, but not coercive questions. If the last three types of questions are incorporated, an interviewer should attempt to return to open-ended cues to facilitate the child sharing his/her detailed narrative.

(I [Interviewer]): "Did someone touch you on your privates?"

(C [Child]): "Yes."

(I): "Tell me about that."

A direct question should not be equated with a leading question. The former style of questioning should be viewed as direct and to the point; the latter presents an expected response and is asked to instill a belief and to produce the desired outcome. Ceci and Bruck (1993) have documented how children can be influenced by misleading questions or by being instilled with a negative stereotype. Other research (Saywitz, Goodman, Nicholas & Moan, 1991) has found that although children are highly resistant to abuse-related misleading questions, the resistance does decrease over time. With this knowledge, an interviewer should be cautious that any direct question is asked in a manner that is not intimidating or influencing; and that once asked, the child is not barraged with the same or similar questions.

Additionally, an interviewer should be aware that younger children may require more directed questions and verbal prompts. Young children are not as skilled as older children and adults at replying to open-ended questions. Their free-recall skills are limited. Thus, younger children require cues or prompts to accurately relay what has occurred in their lives (Saywitz & Goodman, 1993; Pipe, Gee & Wilson, 1993; Fivush & Schwarzmueller, 1995; Hutcheson, Batter, Telfer & Warden, 1995; Toth, 1995).

Furthermore, an interviewer should incorporate a logical sequence and exhaust broader questions before approaching a more direct or closed-ended question. An interviewer should make every attempt to allow a child, and not the interviewer, to introduce the name of the alleged perpetrator.

(I): "Who do you play with?"

(C): "Bob, Mary, and Fred."

(The child has not indicated the alleged perpetrator's name.)

(I): "What do you do with them?"

(C): "We play tag and ghost in the graveyard."

(I): "Who else do you hang out with?"

(C): "No one else."

(I): "Who else is in your neighborhood?"

(C): "Joe and Fran."

(I): "What do you do with them?"

(C): "The same stuff."

(I): "Are there any adults who come around?"

(C): "Um...no."

(I): "Do you know anyone by the name of Todd?"

(C): "I don't think so."

(I): "I heard there was a guy named Todd who lives in your neighborhood. Who is he?"

In the above sequence, it should be noted that open-ended questions were exhausted before direct questions were posed.

If an interviewer needs to ask a more closed-ended question, he/she should make every effort to balance the negative connotation with a positive one.

(I): "What are things that you like to do with Todd?"

(C): "We go to the movies and get ice cream."

(I): "What movies do you see?"

(C): "Cartoons."

(I): "Any other ones?"

(C): "No."

(I): "What kind of ice cream do you like to get?"

(C): "Chocolate."

(I): "What store do you go to?"

(C): "Smith's."

(I):"What are things that you don't like to do with Todd?"

It is the interviewer's responsibility to ask the who, what, where, when, and why/how of the alleged abuse. Children younger than 4 will have greater difficulty with relaying the when and why/how of the situation (Hewitt, 1995). An interviewer needs to be cognizant of the "rules of positive elicitation." These rules are assembled through experience and the work of Walker (1994); Braga and Braga,(1991); Saywitz and Goodman (1996); Myers (1992); Goodman and Bottoms (1993); and Hoorwitz (1993).

RULE 1 - MAKE IT SIMPLE.

An interviewer should use easy words, words with which a child is familiar. An interviewer should avoid using pronouns and words that have a double meaning. Using either can lead to much confusion as to who and what are being addressed in the interview. An interviewer needs to get specific information; vague references make this impossible.

Beyond using uncomplicated and understandable words, the sentences should be simple, especially for younger children. An interviewer should limit each sentence to one thought, as opposed to using a compound sentence. Furthermore, an interviewer should avoid using tag phrases; not only do these complicate the sentence and make it longer, they also can cause the interviewer to ask damaging leading question. A tag phrase could include such utterances as:

"You were at your house, <u>right</u>?"

"You were at your house, <u>weren't you</u>?"

"Where were you? <u>In your house</u>?

The first two insinuate coercion. The last statement would be damaging if the child had not already said he/she was in his/her house.

Another way to simplify questions is to avoid the tag phrase, "do you remember?" This phrase requires the child to take an extra step. First, the child has to recall the information, and then relay it. Additionally, some children will respond negatively based on the rationale, "I didn't forget this, so how could I remember?" Furthermore, this phrase gives the child an escape. Instead of answering the question, the child can simply say he/she does not remember.

RULE 2 - LISTEN AND FOLLOW.

An interviewer should use reflective listening, allowing the child to relay as much information as possible without being bombarded with questions. Simple acknowledgements such as:

"Uh, huh..."

"Okay..."

"Ummm....."

"What else?"

"*(repeating what the child has just relayed)* and..."

These indicate to the child that the interviewer is listening, but the interviewer is not validating the responses nor interjecting questions and new information. Often an interviewer will ask a question that conveys an agenda which he/she is following and that disrespects the direction in which a child was proceeding.

(C): "He touched me."

(I): "What room where you in?"

The child is talking about his/her body and the interviewer has switched to the location of the event.

(C): "It was scary."

(I): "Where did he touch you?"

The child was addressing his/her feelings, and the interviewer remained focused on gathering physical details.

It is one of the interviewer's responsibilities to help the child organize the relaying of the details. Bouncing from one topic to another typically results in confusion, and the child may feel misunderstood or invalidated. This can lead the child to withhold further information.

An interviewer should pace the interview in a manner complementary to that of the child. It is normal and recommended to include pauses and silences instead of constant dialogue. Often, an interviewer will end up asking more focused and directed questions because he/she did not allow the child enough time to collect his/her thoughts and respond.

Another aspect of listening and following up is for the interviewer to repeat and/or capsulize what the child has said. This technique allows the interviewer to clarify misunderstandings. This conveys to the child that the interviewer has been listening and addressing inconsistencies in a positive manner.

(With an older child):

(I): "Okay, so far I have heard that you were with Bob, he touched your breast and your vagina, and now I'm confused. One time I thought I heard you say he did put his finger in you, another time I thought you said no, he didn't. Help me out, I wasn't there. What happened?"

(With a younger child)

(I): "Bob touched your boobie and your vagina. What else did he do?"

This is an excellent way to demonstrate that asking for assistance empowers the child and helps him/her respond to future questions, if appropriate, with, "I don't know." or "I am confused by your question."

Slowing down and repeating the child's words allow the interviewer to gather accurate details the child has relayed. An interviewer should try to get a clear picture of what the child is disclosing. If possible, a child should relay the details of the alleged abuse at least twice. Ceci and Bruck (1993), assert that a child may interpret repeated questions as a signal that his/her first response was not correct. With this in mind, an interviewer should offer an explanation for his/her need to repeat the question.

> (I): "You know, I wasn't listening real well..."

> (I): "I'm confused, tell me one more time..."

> (I): "I wasn't there, and I want to make sure I understand..."

RULE 3 - START WITH ALL THE "W" WORDS BUT ONE.

To avoid getting trapped in more direct and potentially leading questions, an interviewer should make every effort to begin a question with an interrogative:

> "What did he do?" rather than, "Did he touch you?"

> "Who was there?" rather than, "Was your mom there?"

> "How was it for you?" rather than, "Was it scary?"

> "Where did it happen?" rather than, "Did it happen in your bedroom?"

> "When did that happen" rather than, "Did it happen at night?"

> "What did she say to you?" rather than, "Did she say something bad would happen to you?"

The one "w" word that should be avoided is "why." A why question connotes blame. It is important for the interviewer to try to rephrase the question with "how come" or "what," even if it is grammatically incorrect. Furthermore, asking "why" may lead a child to make a leap in understanding something that may be incomprehensible to him/her.

> "How come you were at his house?" rather than, "Why were you at his house?"

> "How come you weren't able to tell someone sooner?" rather than, "Why didn't you tell someone sooner?"

> "How come you didn't tell?" rather than, "Why didn't you tell?"

> "What did you think would happen if you tried to leave?" rather than, "Why didn't you leave?"

> "What was it that made you stay there?" rather than, "Why didn't you leave?"

> "How did you end up alone with her?, rather than "Why were you alone with her?"

RULE 4 - BE AWARE OF CHILDREN'S DIFFICULTY WITH RELATIONAL CONCEPTS.

Relational concepts are time frames, sequences, and prepositions. As discussed, younger children have difficulty relaying when the alleged abuse happened. Similarly, younger children may be challenged by prepositions. By 2 years of age, a child begins to use prepositions, with most of the prepositions incorporated into his/her language by age 5 1/2. Mastery of prepositions does not occur until at least 7 years of age (Walker's discussion of Clark & Clark, 1977, 1994). An interviewer should assess whether the child is developmentally seven or older. If so, a prepositional screening need not to be as detailed as for younger children.

Acquiring information about the timing of the alleged abuse may be a simple task with some children, and arduous with others. An interviewer should help a child narrow in on the time of the alleged abuse.

Similar to the funnel style of inquiry, the interviewer should start his/her questioning with the larger time frames, such as the season of the year, progressing to more specific months, days, and hours. One strategy is for the interviewer to focus on the season or temperature. An interviewer can ask about the clothes the child was wearing, i.e., shorts, sweaters, coats; or ask a child if it was hot or cold outside. An interviewer should be aware of his/her climate patterns. If the temperature is always hot, of course, this type of question will not yield useful information. An interviewer can use picture cards to help a child identify the season. Finally, because children typically equate seasons with people, another approach is to ask the child for the people who were present, i.e., teachers, camp counselors, baby-sitters, or activities that were occurring, i.e., television shows, or family outings.

Another avenue is to focus on holidays. Using picture cards that provide symbols for each holiday (Cage, 1991), including a child's birthday, the interviewer should have the child identify which celebration occurred and which did not. This is only effective with children who know their holidays, and for children whose alleged abuse did not occur over a year or more. This activity also requires a significant amount of concentration and knowledge of prepositions, so it should be used carefully.

Once a seasonal reference is established, the interviewer should attempt to discover the day of the week. Some of the ways to do this are to ask a child whether it was a school day, a day in which mommy/daddy went to work, or a day on which a television program aired. Another tactic is to ask the child if any significant or unique activities occurred that day, such as a field trip, doctor's visit, etc. Also, asking a child about other family members' activities, such as a parent's late-work night or activity night, can facilitate a disclosure.

Interviewers should avoid asking questions regarding "yesterday" or "the day before yesterday." This can be a difficult concept for a child. Similarly, asking a child if the alleged abuse occurred "a long time ago" will not be productive. This concept can mean anything from one hour ago to years ago.

Finally, whether or not the day of the week can be established, an interviewer should inquire about the time of day. An interviewer should simply ask, "What time of day was it?" If the child cannot accurately respond, the interviewer should ask whether it was day or night, or if it was dark or light outside.

The other intricate area of relational concepts is prepositions. In a child abuse investigation, a child will be approached with such concepts as:

inside/outside

over/under

on top of/underneath/next to

first/last

before/after

An interviewer should ascertain whether the child understands these concepts during the rapport assessment phase. This is easily accomplished with an object such as an index card, block, or ring, paper, and a bag. Crayons or other drawing materials are not recommended, since the presence of them may lead a child to want to draw rather than talk. In some situations, the interviewer can make this activity more entertaining by asking the child to demonstrate.

(I): "Suzi, put the card inside the bag."

(The child correctly completes the task)

(I): "Good, now put the card outside the bag."

The action can be rotated between the interviewer and the child.

(I): "Suzi, is my hand under the paper?"

(C): "No."

(I): "Is my hand over the paper?"

(C): "Yes."

The question should be simple and not compound. If the question had been phrased using both options, it is highly likely that the interviewer would either get an affirmative response or the last option.

(I): "Suzi, is my hand on top of or under the paper?"

(C): "Yes" or, "Under the paper."

With prepositions related to sequences, before/after and first/last, the latter are easier for children (Walker, 1994). Again, using an object, paper, and a paper bag can assist the child. An interviewer should place the objects in a row.

(I): "Joe, which one is first in the line?...Which one is last?... Is the bag before the crayon?... What comes after the paper?

Also, the concept of before and after can be presented to the child through several drawings of a snowman being built or the three daily meals with the child asked to place them in the correct sequence.

(I): "What happens before this picture/frame?"

"What meal do you eat first?"

(Child places correct picture in place.)

(I): "What happens after this one?"

"What meal comes after lunch?"

The final relational concept is numbers. A child will be asked for the number of times the alleged abuse happened; and although a child can count, this is not an indication that he/she knows the exact number of occurrences. It is uncommon to find children who recall the exact number of times they were abused unless the abuse was a single episode or of very short duration. Rather, children are better at relaying whether the alleged abuse occurred once, a few times, or many times.

(I): "Did this happen one time?"

(C): "No, lots of times."

(I): "I know it can be hard to know exactly how many times, but would you say more than five times?"

(C): "More than that."

(I): "How many would you say?"

(C): "Twenty-five to thirty times."

(I): "Okay, and what makes you think it was that number?"

(C): "Because it happened lots."

With younger children it is recommended to ask them if it happened one time or lots of times. They are unable to give numbers of times. Furthermore they should not be asked if it happened one time or more than one time. The concept of more than is introduced in third grade mathematics. This concept may be difficult for the child to accurately respond to.

RULE 5 - DON'T ASSUME.

An interviewer should never assume that a word used by the child is either understood by the child or is being used correctly. Children will use words that they have heard without having a coherent understanding of them.

(I): "Do you know how come you are here today?"

(C): "Yeah, I was raped."

(I): "Raped...what does that mean?"

(C): "Bobby touched my coochie."

(Clarification and the gathering of details of the alleged assault follow)

(I): "Mary, how did you learn to call what Bobby did to you 'rape'?"

(C): "My friends at school told me that was what it is called."

Another illustration:

(C) "Something happened between me and Bob."

(I): "What happened?"

(C): "We had sex."

(I): "You know sex means a lot of different things to different people. I want to make sure I truly understand what you are saying. What does it mean to you?"

(C): "He laid on top of me and rubbed his weenie between my legs."

(I): "What else happened?"

(C): "That's all."

(I): "He rubbed his penis between your legs. Did he rub it anywhere else?"

(C): "No."

Beyond the words a child uses to describe actions and body parts, an interviewer should never assume what the child's feelings may have been. Speculating on the child's feelings places the interviewer and the child in an awkward position. By making such conjectures, the interviewer has shifted from being objective to being subjective. Furthermore, if the interviewer's assumptions are erroneous, a child may feel either as though the interviewer does not understand or is assigning feelings to him/her, and the child may feel powerless and withdraw from sharing information.

(I): "Bobby, how are you feeling right now?" rather than "Bobby, you look sad. Are you?"

The last area in which an interviewer should not make assumptions is in the abuse scenario. Although several scenarios have similar components, no two abuses are identical. Thus, assuming the use of threats, or presuming that certain acts occurred in a specific order, will hamper the discovery of the truth.

RULE 6 - CHILDREN CAN BE QUITE LITERAL.

An interviewer should constantly be on guard to how he/she phrases a question. "Improper" phrasing can lead to a child omitting important information or providing an inconsistent answer.

(I): "Did this happen when you were in day care?"

(C): "No."

Later in the interview, it was discovered that the child called his day-care "school."

(I): "Did you drive there?"

(C): "No, Tom did."

The child is accurate in who was responsible for driving to the destination.

(I): "Did you touch Tina?"

(C): "No"

(I): "Did Tina have you touch her?"

(C): "Yes."

This last case illustrates how a child knows who is responsible for the action that occurred.

An interviewer should periodically assess the reason for a child's omission or inconsistency. Often, it is the result of the interviewer's own limitations in questioning.

RULE 7 - AVOID THE WORLD OF MAKE-BELIEVE TALK.

An interviewer should abstain from using phrases such as magical, pretend, imagine, and make believe. Introducing these words may discredit the child's disclosure.

Furthermore, an interviewer should never introduce a discussion topic as being a game.

(I):"Now we're going to play a game. Put the card under the bag."

Although it makes the task appear friendlier, the question may arise as to when the game playing ceased and the reality of disclosure began.

RULE 8 - AVOID ASKING FOR PERMISSION.

This rule appears contradictory since empowerment of the child has been advocated. However, an interviewer can get into a predicament if he/she asks the child for consent to enter into specific dialogue or activities. Basically, an interviewer should question him/herself, "Can I handle a negative response. Will it hamper my discovering the truth?"

(I): "Can we talk about touching now?"

(C): "No."

Or:

(I): "Is it okay for me to ask you a few questions?"

(C): "No."

To proceed, the interviewer must invalidate the child's response. This is unempowering. In the investigative interview, certain areas must be addressed. Giving a child an apparent option to proceed is not being genuine. An interviewer can phrase the question so it appears to be a topic that can be addressed in a joint manner:

"Now we're going to talk about touching," rather than, "Can we talk about touching?"

"Let's look at a picture," rather than,"Is it okay if I show you a picture?"

"Let's talk about it," rather than, "Can you tell me about it?"

These statements should be followed by the interviewer promptly engaging in the dialogue or activity.

RULE 9 - BE AWARE OF BODY LANGUAGE.

Not all language is verbal. Body language sometimes speaks louder than words. An interviewer needs to be aware of what his/her body is saying. An interviewer should assume a position and try to retain it. Leaning forward and backward can influence what a child says, as can a nod of the interviewer's head. An interviewer should pay attention to his/her body movement and adjust it accordingly.

When conducting an extensive investigative interview, the interviewer needs to be attuned to several issues related to questioning and language. An interviewer needs to be aware not only of his/her spoken word and style but also of his/her body language. An interviewer also has to be cognizant of the child's capabilities and limitations, and proceed appropriately.

REFERENCES:

Boat, B., & Everson, M. (1986). *Using anatomical dolls: Guidelines for interviewing young children in sexual abuse investigations.* University of North Carolina, Chapel Hill: Department of Psychiatry.

Braga, J., & Braga, L. (1991). Notes from a workshop conducted at the national symposium on child sexual abuse. Huntsville, AL.

Cage, R. (1991). Personal communication.

Ceci, S., & Bruck, M. (1993). The suggestibility of the child witness: A historical review and synthesis. *Psychological Bulletin, 113,* 403-439.

Ceci, S., & Bruck, M. (1995). *Jeopardy in the courtroom: A scientific analysis of children's testimony.* Washington, DC: American Psychological Association.

Clark, H., & Clark, E. (1977). *Psychology and Language.* NY: Harcourt Brace Javonovich.

Faller, K. (1990). Types of questions for assessing allegation of sexual abuse. *The APSAC Advisor, 3*(2), 5-7.

Fivush, R., & Schwarzmueller, A. (1995). Say it once again: Effects of repeated questions on children's event recall. *Journal of Traumatic Stress, 8*(4), 555-580.

Goodman, G., & Bottoms, B. (Eds.) (1993). *Child victims, child witnesses: Understanding and improving testimony.* New York: Guilford Press.

Goodman, G., Bottoms, B., Schwartz-Kenney, B., & Rudy, L. (1991). Children's testimony about a stressful event: Improving children's reports. *Journal of Narrative and Life History, 1,* 69-99.

Hewitt, S. (1995). *Small voices ... Big wound: Assessing and managing cases of sexually abused young children.* Seminar coordinated by The Creche Child and Family Centre and the Catholic Children's Aid Society of Metropolitan Toronto. Toronto, Canada.

Hoorwitz, A.N. (1993). *The clinical detective: Techniques in the evaluation of sexual abuse.* New York: Norton.

Hutcheson, G., Baxter, J., Telfer, K., & Warden, D. (1995). Child witness statement quality. *Law and Human Behavior, 19*(6), 631-659.

Lamb, M., Sternberg, K., & Esplin, P. (1995). Making children into competent witnesses: Reactions to the amicus brief in re Michael's *Psychology, Public Policy, and Law, 1*(2), 411-428.

Myers, J. (1992). *Legal issues in child abuse and neglect.* Thousand Oaks, CA: Sage Publications.

Pipe, M., Gee, S., & Wilson, C. (1993). Cues, props, and context: Do they facilitate children's event reports? In G. Goodman, & B. Bottoms (Eds.), *Child victims, child witnesses: Understanding and improving testimony* (pp. 25-46). New York: Guilford Press.

Saywitz, K., Goodman, G., Nicholas, G., & Moan, S. (1991). Children's memory for genital exam: Implications for child sexual abuse. *Journal of Consulting and Clinical Psychology, 59,* 682-691.

Saywitz, K., & Goodman, G. (1993). Interviewing children in and out of court: Current research and practical implications. National Center on Child Abuse and Neglect grant.

Saywitz, K., & Goodman, G. (1996). Interviewing children in and out of court: Current research and practical implications. In J. Briere, L. Berliner, J. Bulkley, C. Jenny, & T. Reid (Eds.), *The APSAC Handbook on Child Maltreatment.* Thousand Oaks, CA: Sage Publications.

Toth, P. (1995). Dialogue from author's training: *Interviewing sexually abused children.* Huntsville, AL: Office of Victims of Crime Federal Training Day.

Walker, A. (1994). *Handbook on questioning children: A linguistic perspective.* Washington, DC: American Bar Association. National Legal Resource Center for Child Advocacy and Protection, Center on Children and the Law.

Chapter 5

FICTITIOUS VERSUS VALID REPORTS

The believability of child abuse allegations is a dominant and critical issue. An interviewer should be informed of the research and the various models of disclosure analysis and substantiation. An interviewer should know that an unsubstantiated report and a false report are two disparate findings. The former indicates that either the allegation was found to not be true or that there was not enough evidence to accurately confirm or nullify the report of the alleged abuse. The latter implies that following a thorough investigation the evidence did not confirm the allegation.

The possibilities for an allegation of child sexual abuse (Nurcombe, 1986; Yuille, 1988; Green, 1986; Jones & McGraw, 1986; Bernet, 1993; Faller, 1988; Gardner, 1987: & Gardner, 1989) are:

1. The report is a truthful and accurate account;

2. The report is an accurate account of behaviors/symptoms; however, it is based on a caregiver's/reporting source's hypervigilance, overanxiousness, and/or misinterpretation or miscommunication;

3. The report stemmed from a copycat phenomenon;

4. The report is intentionally fabricated and is of a malicious, retaliatory, or secondary gain nature;

5. The report is fraudulent and is based on a third-party influence; or

6. The report is erroneous and is based on sexual fantasies.

Research has found between two and eight percent of allegations to be fabricated. (Peters, 1976; Goodwin, Sahd, & Rada, 1978; Jones & McGraw, 1986; and Faller, 1988). However, an interviewer needs to be aware that children are more likely to deny true abuse than to make false accusations. (Faller, 1988; Chaffin & Lawson, 1992; and Sorenson & Snow, 1991).

Valid allegations will appear in two forms, accurate accounts of abuse and accurate accounts of behaviors related to abuse. In the latter, a well-intentioned individual, typically a mandated reporter, makes a referral based on observable behavior. In some cases, a hypervigilant parent may misperceive a child's behaviors or comments as abuse and report accordingly. In both cases the referral source is not malicious but rather sincerely believes that the alleged abuse has occurred.

Fictitious reports come from a variety of sources. Although the phenomenon of copycat reports and sexual fantasies has been proposed (Green, 1986) insignificant data exist to support these conjectures.

Intentional fabrication on the part of a child has been studied. There is no evidence to indicate that children are any more or less apt to lie than adults (Berliner, 1988). Myers (1994) reports that fabrication in young children is uncommon. By comparison, Faller (1988) and Goodwin, et al., (1978), found that the most common age group to fabricate reports is older adolescents. However, it was found that this population commonly had a history of abuse or emotional stress and would make the false allegation for retaliatory and secondary gains. However, this research does not show that most adolescents' allegations are fictional.

False reports based on third-party influence can arise from two sources, vengeful parties and misguided interviewers. Gardner (1987) proposed a parental alienation syndrome in which one parent coaches or leads a nonabused child to report and believe he/she was abused. Additionally, Loftus (1993) has documented cases in which improper interviewing strategies have led to the creation of abuse memory and distorted recollections of abuse.

No matter what the source of the referral, an exhaustive and objective investigation and review of the case is needed. The child and all parties, nonabusing family members, collateral sources, and the alleged abuser(s), need to be interviewed. If there is evidence, it needs to be gathered and corroborated. As important as the disclosures and confessions are, so too are corroborating evidence regarding behavioral changes, the child's attempted and completed disclosures to others, and either eyewitnesses or witnesses who can verify time frames of perpetrator access. The above data need to be analyzed in a competent investigation.

Not only should the entire investigative interview be examined, but the child's disclosure(s) should be analyzed. Several guidelines for assessing the credibility of a child's account have been developed (Everson, 1991; Jones & McGraw, 1986; Marxsen, Yuille, Nisbet, 1995; Corwin, 1988; Raskin & Esplin, 1991; Yuille, 1988; and Bradford, 1994). The following criteria are compiled from their works. As is valid in indicators of child sexual abuse, it is important for the interviewer to focus not on a single factor as definitive, but rather on the combination and cluster of indicators.

CHARACTERISTICS OF THE CHILD'S DISCLOSURE:

    1. Explicit detailed account. Does the child provide sufficient detail that is set in a compatible spacial-physical context? Does the child provide a thorough description of the interactions? However, does the child admit lacking complete memory of all

infinitesimal details? Does the child have details of sexual acts of which he/she would not have prior or such detailed knowledge?

2. Idiosyncratic and sensory-motor details. Does the child share unusual and peripheral details? Does the child provide any reproduction of dialogue that may have occurred? Does the child incorrectly describe an act/detail that he/she misunderstood due to lack of experience/knowledge, i.e., "He peed white," rather than, "He ejaculated." Does the child include external details that he/she associates with the abuse, such as conversations and grooming patterns?

3. Description based on child's point of reference. Are the details based on a first-person account or a second-person account? Does the child produce a spontaneous reproduction of the event, rather than a rehearsed description? Can the child describe his/her feelings at the time of the event? Does the child infer the alleged perpetrator's feelings/motivation?

4. Child's vocabulary and sentence structure are congruent with his/her age. Are the child's words developmentally appropriate? This does not mean that if a child uses the anatomical name for a body part that he/she is fabricating. It can be helpful to ask a parent before the interview what words the child uses to describe genitalia and other body parts and actions.

5. Child's affect is either appropriate or congruent with his/her coping style. Not all children demonstrate fear, sadness, and anger when relaying the details of the alleged abuse. Some have become accommodated to it and accept it as a routine part of their lives (Summitt, 1983). An interviewer cannot determine the validity of an allegation based on the child's presenting affect.

6. Child provides consistency in the core elements of the abuse. The child usually does not have complete recollection of all details, but rather the central elements of the alleged abuse should remain consistent. Does the child spontaneously correct him/herself?

7. Psychological response to abuse. Although no universally agreed upon child sexual abuse syndrome exists, does the child portray some symptoms synonymous with those that known sexually abused children demonstrate? Does the child feel responsibility for the abuse, the feelings he/she may have had, for the benefits which he/she received? Does the child attempt to pardon or justify the perpetrator's actions?

8. Pattern of abuse and timing of disclosure. Are there common threads between this report and others? Have other children been molested by the alleged perpetrator? What precipitated the child's disclosure?

9. Element of secrecy. What overt or covert strategies were applied to ensure the concealment of the abuse?

10. Coercion and threats. What methods were employed by the alleged perpetrator to ensure the continuance of the alleged abuse and the child's involvement?

An interviewer should ask him/herself these questions when analyzing the collective data. (See Chapter 15 for a structured guide.)

One component of a child's disclosure that has received significant attention is inconceivable statements. Everson (1995) labeled them fantasy-like statements; Dalenberg (1996) classified them as fantastic elements in disclosure. Inconceivable statements are those that seem absurd and highly unlikely.

"After he touched me, I beat him up so bad."

"Mickey Mouse abused me."

"It was like I was in a dream."

Inconceivable statements can decrease the child's credibility in the eyes of the interviewer and the system. They can also lead to dismissal of the conceivable details that the child has disclosed.

Everson (1995) and MacFarlane (1996) proposed several plausible explanations for fantasy-like/inconceivable statements.

1. The truth.

2. Misperception or miscommunication due to the child's development or to the child fitting the experience into an existing schematic. For example, a child might relay that a knife was inserted into her vagina when she was penetrated with a finger. The experience was painful and the child has learned that knives can hurt, thus the child connects the pain to a knife. Another example is a child disclosing that the alleged perpetrator urinated on him/her, when the alleged perpetrator ejaculated.

3. Trauma affects memory. A child's coping strategy during the abuse or the way in which the abuse was processed and stored may impact the disclosure. Strauss (1996) found that adult victims of severe physical abuse experienced time-limited distortions. Furthermore, a child may attempt to fill in the gaps in his/her broken memory, thus creating an inconceivable statement.

4. The use of drugs and alcohol during the abuse can lead to incoherence on the part of the child, thus leading to bizarre statements.

5. A deliberate attempt by the perpetrator to discredit a child's disclosure. Some perpetrators may dress in costumes or conduct a pseudo-ritual to contaminate the credibility of the child's disclosure.

6. A child may incorporate a threat as if it were carried out. If a perpetrator has threatened a child, and the child discloses, he/she may believe that the threat will come true. For example, a 4 year old girl had been told that her baby sister would be killed if she told. Following her disclosure, she informed the interviewer that a baby girl was buried in the backyard.

7. A child's mastery over fear or anxiety. Following a solid disclosure, a child might tell the interviewer, "And then I kicked him and beat him up."In reality, this did not occur, but rather the child had wished he/she had been able to protect him/herself or seek vengeance.

8. Interviewer error. Dalenberg (1996) reports that fantastic elements are not related to leading questions. If an interviewer has preconceptions of how the child's abuse occurred, he/she can contribute to the fantasy-like statement. Furthermore, if an interviewer asks the child to speculate or creates an atmosphere of accusation a fantastic quality of disclosure can arise. (MacFarlane, 1996)

9. An escalating lie or attention-seeking mechanism. This is seen in a child who did not believe people would care that he/she was fondled so he/she embellished his/her allegation.

10. A child being psychotic.

Should an interviewer respond to an inconceivable statement or should it be ignored? The jury is still out. Experience has found that asking about it as an interviewer would any other topic has been appropriate. Dalenberg (1996) and Dalenberg and O'Neel (1992) found that more inconceivable/fantastic elements are found in the disclosures of more severe abuse, which can be corroborated (perpetrator confession, medical evidence, eyewitness), than in disclosures that were deliberately fabricated or unsupported. However, the findings warrant caution. An interviewer should not decide that an inconceivable statement accompanying a disclosure automatically makes the allegation valid. Rather, an interviewer should be aware that the presence of an inconceivable statement does not automatically negate the entire disclosure.

To ensure an unprejudiced investigation, in which every conceivable step will be taken to arrive at the truth, a meticulous review of not only the child's disclosure but all aspects of the case should occur. This should happen immediately after the child's disclosure and throughout the investigation as new evidence is obtained. An interviewer and the multidisciplinary team should examine every hypothesis.

REFERENCES:

Berliner, L. (1988). Deciding whether a child has been sexually abused. In E.B. Nicholson & J. Bulkley (Eds.), *Sexual abuse allegations in custody and visitation cases* (pp. 48-69). Washington, DC: American Bar Association. National Legal Resource Center for Child Advocacy and Protection, Center on Children and the Law.

Bernet, W. (1993). False statements and the differential diagnosis of abuse allegations. *Journal of the American Academy of child and Adolescent Psychiatry, 32*(5) 903-909.

Bradford, R. (1994). Developing an objective approach to assessing allegations of sexual abuse. *Child Abuse Review, 3,* 93-101.

Chaffin, M., & Lawson, L. (1992). False negatives in sexual abuse disclosure interviews. *Journal of Interpersonal Violence, 7,* 532-542.

Corwin, David. (1988). Early diagnosis of child sexual abuse: Diminishing the lasting effects. In *Lasting Effects of Child Sexual Abuse,* G. Wyatt and G. Powell (Eds.). Thousand Oaks, CA: Sage Publications.

Dalenberg, C. (1996). Fantastic elements in child disclosure of abuse. *APSAC Advisor, 9*(2), 1-10.

Dalenberg, C., & O'Neel, K. (1992). *True and false allegations of physical abuse: The role of the mother in constructing a believable story.* San Diego Conference on Responding to Child Maltreatment.

Everson, M. (1991). *Factors for assessing the credibility of a child's report of sexual abuse.* University of North Carolina, Chapel Hill: Dept. of Psychiatry.

Everson, M. (1995). *Understanding unusual, improbable, and fantasy-like statements in children's accounts of abuse.* San Diego Conference on Responding to Child Maltreatment.

Faller, K. (1988). Criteria for judging the credibility of children's statements about their sexual abuse. *Child Welfare, 67,* 389-401.

Gardner, R.A. (1987). Sex abuse legitimacy scale. Cresskill, NJ: *Creative Therapeutics.*

Gardner, R.A. (1989). Differentiating between bona fide and fabricated allegations of sexual abuse of children. *Journal of the Academy of Matrimonial Lawyers, 5,* 1-25.

Goodwin, J., Sahd, D., & Rada, R. (1978). Incest hoax: False accusations, false denials. *Bulletin of the American Academy of Psychiatry and the Law, 6,* 269-276.

Green, A. (1986). True and false allegations of sexual abuse in custody disputes. *Journal of the American Academy of Child Psychiatry, 25,* 449-456.

Jones, David P.H., & J. Melbourne McGraw. (1986). *Draft: Reliable and fictitious accounts of sexual abuse to children.*

Loftus, E. (1993). The reality of repressed memories. *American Psychologist, 48,* 518-537.

MacFarlane, Kee. (1996). Presentation for the Children's International Institute's Five Day Advanced Forensic Interviewing Clinic. Los Angeles, CA.

Marxsen D., Yuille, J., & Nisbet, M. (1995). The complexities of eliciting and assessing children's statements. *Psychology, Public Policy, and the Law, 1*(2), 450-460.

Myers, J. (1994). Can we believe what children say about sexual abuse? *The APSAC Advisor, 7*(1), 5-6.

Nurcombe, B. (1986). The child as witness: Competency and credibility. *Journal of the American Academy of Child Psychiatry, 25,* 473-480.

Peters, J. (1976). Children who are victims of sexual assault and the psychology of offenders. *American Journal of Psychotherapy, 30,* 398-421.

Raskin, D., & Esplin, P. (1991). Statement of validity assessment: Interview procedures and content analysis of children's statement of sexual abuse. *Behavioral Assessment, 13,* 265-291.

Sorenson, T., & Snow, B. (1991). How children tell: The process of disclosure in child sexual abuse. *Child Welfare, 70,* 3-15.

Strauss, K. (1996). *Differential diagnosis of battered women through psychological testing: Personality disorder or post traumatic stress syndrome.* Unpublished doctoral dissertation. California School of Professional Psychology.

Summitt, R. (1983). The child sexual abuse accommodation syndrome. *Child Abuse and Neglect, 7,* 177-192.

Yuille, J.C. (1988). The systematic assessment of children's testimony. *Canadian Psychology, 29,* 247-262.

Chapter 6

INTERVIEWER CHARACTERISTICS

Crucial to an investigative interview is the interviewer. It is imperative that the interviewer possess the essential qualifications and characteristics. If the interviewer is not well-suited for the role, there is a strong likelihood that the interviews will fail. Agencies hiring mandates and established guidelines, such as the American Professional Society on the Abuse of Children (1990), are beneficial when developing professional expectations for the interviewer.

Objectivity is the first quality required in an interviewer. (Myers, 1994; Faller, 1996). Professionals and researchers (Gardner, 1991; Gardner, 1992; Quinn, 1989; and Ceci, 1993) have brought attention to the possibility that child abuse investigators and interviewers may operate in an overzealous fashion. It is important to approach the interview in an objective manner not as a mission to prove the alleged abuse but as a mission to discover the truth. An interviewer should begin an interview, remain in the interview and close the interview with an open mind. Two valuable questions an interviewer should pose are: "Through my mannerisms, do I subtly bribe, threaten, or coerce this child?" and, "Do I lend credibility or withhold credibility from this investigation?"

It is important for the interviewer to remain open to the possibility that the alleged abuse may not have occurred. Adopting the following philosophy can be advantageous: Any child who comes to the system's attention has a problem. That problem may be that he/she was sexually abused; that someone has coerced the child into reporting that another person has molested him/her; that the child was angry and is retaliating through a false disclosure of abuse; or that the reporting source misinterpreted behaviors and/or symptoms. It is the interviewer's responsibility to gather the facts and assist the multidisciplinary team in arriving at a plausible explanation for the report and facilitating the subsequent intervention.

If the alleged abuse has occurred, it is essential that the child and nonoffending family members receive the necessary services to facilitate their recovery. Furthermore, the identified perpetrator needs to be held responsible for his/her actions. If the report is found to be false, it is crucial that the accused individual be exonerated.

Another aspect of objectivity is the interviewer's personal history with and attitudes toward the victims, nonoffending parents, and perpetrators. An interviewer should take personal inventory of his/her past and attitudes and question him/herself. "Will my beliefs affect my professionalism?" and, "Will my issues get in the way of my discovering the truth?"

An interviewer should not become consumed with having a "perfect record" with regard to disclosures. An interviewer's credibility increases as the ratio between disclosures and nondisclosures is naturally balanced, and reflects national and regional trends.

Another characteristic is for the interviewer to be rehabilitative. The investigative interview should be viewed as a child's gateway to recovery. Healing cannot truly begin until the facts of the abuse are disclosed. Logic says it is easier to relay potentially embarrassing information in an environment that is nurturing and rehabilitative. Beyond the physical constraints, creating such an environment is the interviewer's responsibility.

It is important for an interviewer to know that in typical abuse situations more has occurred than is initially reported. An interviewer needs to provide an arena in which the child can disclose as much as possible. This is not to say that every investigative interview will yield all the details of every child's abuse. Children have reasons for withholding information.

Remember the need for the balance of forensic and therapeutic. An interviewer should be careful to avoid being interrogative and requiring only the facts unaccompanied by feelings and perceptions. Although fact-gathering is critical, it is just as vital to validate the child's feeling. By asking related questions, the child may disclose more details. The interviewer should frequently ask the child, "How did you feel?" and, "How are you feeling now?"

Furthermore, if a child says, "I do not want to talk about this anymore," the interviewer should heed this statement instead of explaining how important it is to talk about it now. The conversation should shift to processing the child's present feelings.

(C): "I don't want to talk about it."

(I): "Okay...How are you feeling right now?"

(C): "Yucky."

(I): "I can guess, but what makes you feel yucky?"

(C): "When I think about what she did."

(I): "Help me out..."

(C): "Well, she made me feel yucky."

(I): "How so?"

(C): "When she would touch me."

43

Nine times out of ten the conversation will soon return to the disclosure. However, if it does not, the interviewer should relay to the child the importance of sharing the truth.

Creating a nurturing environment also means an interviewer should pay attention to his/her body position in relationship to the child. Sitting directly across from the child, whether a desk is present or not, could add to an interrogative/confrontational climate. Rather, physical barriers should not directly separate the interviewer and the child, and assuming a position similar to that of living-room settings, of forty-five- to ninety-degree angles between the interviewer and the child, is beneficial. However, with younger children sitting at a child-size table can facilitate drawing. If a table is used, every effort should be made to have the child and the interviewer sit on the same side or on two adjacent sides.

Interpersonal boundaries should also be respected. If an interviewer sits across the room from the child, it may appear that he/she is not interested or is disgusted by the child; and if they are too close, it may make the child uncomfortable.

It is necessary to remember that being nurturing does not automatically imply cuddling and interpretive free-play activities. Quite the contrary; an interviewer should be concerned about physical contact. It is strongly recommended that an interviewer avoid touching a child who has been allegedly sexually abused. An innocent touch to a child who has been abused may have a completely different meaning than a touch to a child who has not. A simple reassuring hand on the shoulder may bring comfort to a child who has not been abused; the same touch to an abused child may trigger a response to the original abuse or may make him/her believe that the interviewer is trying to be sexual with him/her. If that child has a fear response, disclosure is very unlikely.

Secondly, children who have been sexually abused frequently have difficulty establishing appropriate boundaries and once they have been touched, they may try to seduce the interviewer. If they have associated affection and touch with sexuality, these children may try to please the interviewer.

Browne and Finklehor (1986) explained these response patterns as traumatic sexualization. Traumatic sexualization results in sexually abused children either correlating sex with rewards or sex with fright. In the former, perpetrators often reward sexually abused children for sexual behavior. This reward can be materialistic and/or attention/affection. As a result, sexually abused children may use sexual behavior to get needs met and to manipulate others. Because of the attention/affection they receive, sexually abused children give distorted importance and meaning to their anatomy.

Sexually abused children's sexuality can become traumatized when frightening and unpleasant memories become associated in the child's mind with sexual activity and even benign touches.

However, an interviewer should be prepared for the possibility of a child either touching him/her, significantly crossing personal boundaries, or climbing onto the interviewer's lap. When this occurs, an interviewer should be careful not to respond in an alarming or reprimanding manner. Rather, asking the child to remove himself/herself is the best approach.

> (I): "I have a hard time talking to you when you are so close to my face. Please sit here, so I can see you."

Another area for potential boundary conflict is the introduction of play. Engaging a child in play/imagination activities can decrease the credibility of the investigation. Play activities may also act as an escape device for the child.

Beyond an objective and rehabilitative stance, an interviewer must be able to deal with pain and trauma (Hindman, 1987; James, 1989; and Sgroi, 1982). Children follow non-verbal cues. Actions speak louder than words. It is said that words comprise just 10 percent of our communication, while sounds make up 30 percent and body language 60 percent. If the child sees an interviewer wincing or trying to divert the interview from uncomfortable subjects, the child will conclude, "I'd better be silent; I don't want to disgust this person who is paying attention to me."

When does a child ever get 30 to 45 minutes of an adult's undivided attention? Often, children do not want to sabotage the attention they are receiving, and they will shift topics if they realize the interviewer is becoming uncomfortable. Other thoughts the child might have include: "I really must be bad if what happened even 'grosses' this person out, and this is a person who is supposed to be able to deal with this kind of stuff." Or finally, "I'm bad, I'm in trouble, this person is horrified with me." Sometimes, a child is only looking for an excuse not to disclose. An interviewer needs to be careful not to provide one.

Just as it is important for an interviewer to be able to deal with pain and trauma, he/she must be able to deal with discussions related to sexuality (Hindman, 1987). If an interviewer becomes embarrassed with using sexual terms, whether they are the scientific terms or the slang that the child uses, or unordinary sexual practices, a child will probably react similarly.

Another characteristic of a good interviewer is his/her ability to communicate with children and adolescents. "Is this interviewer comfortable with the age range with whom he/she is interviewing?" If an interviewer has difficulty talking with one age range, an interview can become nonproductive. If an interviewer uses big words with a small child, the child may become confused. Or if an interviewer talks in a childlike tone with an adolescent, the adolescent may refuse to discuss information. This refers to nonverbal cues too. If an interviewer sits rigidly or sits in a chair with legs crossed, a young child may think, "This person really isn't on my level and doesn't want to talk." If an interviewer asks an older adolescent to sit cross-legged on the floor, the adolescent may feel belittled.

An interviewer should be cognizant of praising the child. If a child receives too much praise, he/she may try to please the interviewer to receive the desired attention and praise, and suggestibility may occur. It is useful for the interviewer to praise the child's actions rather than the child's being. Examples of this include:

"The drawing is good" rather than, "You're a good drawer."

"You know your colors" or "Right" rather than, "You're smart."

An interviewer needs to be cautious not to create the appearance or reality that a child would say anything to receive affirmation and attention from the interviewer.

Another vital part of the interview is realizing that the disclosure process is complicated. As a child is entertaining the option of disclosing the abuse, he/she may be replaying in his/her mind what the perpetrator said regarding the consequences of disclosing. This is similar to daytime soap operas that portray an individual reliving a volatile conversation at the exact moment they are making a crucial decision. Understandably the child may be concerned about whether the threats will be carried out. The child may be protecting the family by refusing to report, or he/she may have tried to protect younger siblings from abuse by allowing the perpetrator to continue abusing him/her.

An interviewer cannot change this for the child, but he/she should be aware that disclosing is not a simple decision for a child. Many children just want the abuse to stop. They do not wish for their perpetrator to be punished or for the threats to become reality. It is important for the interviewer to be empathic. The child may be confused and frightened not only by how the perpetrator maintained the abusive relationship, but by the investigating system. The interviewer knows the system is there to benefit the child, but the child may not be aware of this.

Additionally, an interviewer should never present him/herself to the child as needing anything. Such comments as, "Do me a favor," or, "Make me a picture," should be avoided. Rather, dialogue that sets up a partnership is preferable: "Let's draw." Again, it is important that the interviewer not require the child to please him/her. Once a child seeks to please the interviewer, the factual nature of his/her account can be called into question.

Finally, an interviewer should be able to effectively communicate and respesent the other members of the multidisciplinary team. It is recommended that only one person conduct an interview. This is not to discourage the use of multidisciplinary teams. However, having one person do the interview on behalf of law enforcement, child protective services, and the prosecutor's office can be advantageous for the child. Having one interviewer does not create the feeling of the child being "ganged up upon" by the interviewers. One individual can successfully conduct the interview on behalf of the other professionals.

REFERENCES:

American Professional Society on the Abuse of Children. (1990). *Guidelines for psychosocial evaluation of suspected sexual abuse in young children.* Chicago: American Professional Society on the Abuse of Children.

Browne, A., & Finkelhor, D. (1986). Impact of child sexual abuse. A review of the research. *Psychological Bulletin, 99,* 66-77.

Ceci, S. (1993). *From the mouths of babes.* ABC-TV 20/20 News Magazine.

Faller, K. (1996). Evaluating children suspected of having been sexually abused: *The APSAC Study Guides, 2.* Thousand Oaks, CA: Sage Publications.

Gardner, R.A. (1991). *Sex abuse hysteria, Salem witch trials revisited.* Cresskill, NJ: Creative Therapeutics.

Gardner, R.A. (1992). *True and false accusations of child sexual abuse.* Cresskill, NJ: Creative Therapeutics.

Hindman, J. (1987). *Step by step: Sixteen steps toward legally sound sexual abuse investigations.* Ontario, OR: Alexandria Press.

James, B. (1989). *Treating traumatized children: New insights and creative interventions.* Lexington, MA: Lexington Books.

Myers, J. (1994). *The backlash: Child protection under fire.* Thousand Oaks, CA: Sage Publications.

Quinn, K. (1989). Resolved: Child sexual abuse is over-diagnosed: Affirmative. *Journal of American Academy of Child and Adolescent Psychiatry, 28,* 789-790.

Sgroi, S. (1982). *Handbook of clinical intervention in child sexual abuse.* Lexington, MA: Lexington Books.

Chapter 7

THE INTERVIEWING ROOM AND INTERVIEWING AIDS

An interviewing room should be comfortable but not overwhelming (National Network of Children's Advocacy Centers, 1994; MacFarlane, 1995; Myers, 1992). In designing an interview room, it is important to look at the dimensions, the size and type of furniture, the type and placement of audiovisual equipment, the variety and placement of interviewing aids, and decorations. When possible, there should be two interviewing rooms, one for younger children and one for older children/adolescents.

A child's fairy tale can be instructional in the development of the interviewing room. The story of Goldilocks and the three bears teaches us that appropriate-size furniture generates comfort. Accordingly, the furniture in the young children's interviewing room should be young-child size. Older children's furniture should fit them. The atmosphere and the furniture should emphasize a homelike, child-friendly ambience versus a business environment. Having a room set up like a living room is much more conducive to an interview than two chairs separated by a desk.

The size of the room should also be carefully considered. The room should be comfortable but not enormous nor full of distractions. In the children's interviewing room, there should be space for a small table with a few small chairs, a little sofa, and an out-of-child's reach cupboard or storage space. In the older children's interviewing room an arrangement of comfortable chairs and/or a small sofa arrangement and storage space is beneficial. However, a writing surface should be available, whether a clipboard, folding table, television tray, or some other item.

Both rooms should be free of toys and activities. Toys can distract. Use murals, stencils, playful pictures painted on the walls and brightly painted furniture to create a child-friendly environment. Toys that will be used as aids during the interview should be in the storage areas. These should be easily accessible to the interviewer but not the child (Jones & McQuiston, 1988; and Barker, 1990).

An interviewing room should be uninterruptible. There should be no telephone in the room to disrupt an interview. The traffic flow should be considered if it is an office in which people are likely to walk through or is adjacent to a busy hallway. If a child hears conversations outside the room, he/she may believe several people are eavesdropping and may be less likely to disclose; thus, keeping the room private and secluded can have its benefits. If a distraction-free room is impossible, enforce quiet in the adjoining halls during interviews.

Similarly, the proximity of the interviewing room to the waiting room is of critical concern. The expression "the walls have ears" is familiar. If the room is near where a nonabusing parent is, the child may feel that his/her voice may travel, thus impeding the likelihood of a disclosure.

Aids and toys used in the interview should receive the same careful attention. Some authors (Barker, 1990: and National Network of Children's Advocacy Centers, 1994) advocate a wide variety of toys placed in the room, so the child has several objects to play with. Others (Spaulding, 1987; Mead, Balch, & Maggio, 1985; and Jones & McQuiston, 1988) stress the need for few play materials, only those necessary for the facilitation of dialogue. In agreement with the latter opinion and through experience, the following interviewing tools have been found to be advantageous:

1. Three sets of the anatomically detailed dolls, with each set including mother, father, son, daughter, grandfather, and grandmother representing Caucasian, African-American, and Hispanic populations. If finances allow, duplicate sets should be available. This will assist in multi-victim/multi-perpetrator cases. It also guarantees that an interview room is fully equipped.

2. Three sets of regular play dolls. Practitioners and personal experience have found that having non-anatomical dolls, such as Cabbage Patch or rag dolls, in addition to anatomically detailed dolls grants the child another disclosure tool. This type of doll provides one more way to demonstrate that the interview was not biased. (Jones & McQuiston, 1988; and Britton & O'Keefe, 1991).

3. Anatomical drawings (Groth & Stevenson, 1990).

Like the dolls, the drawings, which provide a front and a backview of young children through the elderly for Caucasian and African-American populations, can clarify information regarding the alleged abuse. If an interviewer is concerned about the appearance of the Groth drawings, other options for anatomical drawings include gingerbread drawings of the male and female, and the drawings where the genetalia is covered with a swimsuit.

4. An assortment of crayons, markers, and paper. These may be used for free drawing or for drawing pictures of the alleged crime scene(s).

5. Feeling cards. For younger children the concept of feelings can be difficult. Having simple pictures of faces that represent various feelings can assist a child.

6. Competency charts (Cage, 1991). Using color and animal charts can assist a child distinguish true statements from false. (This will be discussed further in Chapter 10.)

7. Seasonal cards.To assist a child with time frames, picture cards can be beneficial. Simply using the front of greeting cards to depict the holidays and seasons can facilitate a child disclosing the time frame of the alleged abuse.

Research (Conte, Sorenson, Fogarty, & Dalla Rosa, 1991; and Kendall-Tackett & Watson, 1991) shows that the anatomically-detailed dolls are the most widely used tools by professionals; in the first study, 92 percent of the respondents reported using dolls, and in the latter study, a significant number of the mental health providers and 62 percent of law enforcement professionals surveyed reported using dolls. However, several jurisdictions have curtailed use of the dolls because of their controversial nature. As is seen in the majority of decisions regarding investigative interviews, the decision to incorporate the dolls should be a multidisciplinary decision. Although infrequently utilized in the interviews in which the author has participated and supervised, dolls are a resource, thus relevant literature has been reviewed and related training has been obtained.

Experience has found that the anatomical drawings yield a productive interview. Research has found that the drawings are the second most widely used tool; two-thirds of those polled by Conte, et al. (1991) and 47 percent of those polled by Kendall-Tackett & Watson (1991) used them. There has been far less research on the anatomically detailed drawings. One study (Steward, 1989) found the drawings to be better than just dialogue but not preferable than any other tool. Furthermore, research and experience have found the drawings less helpful in demonstrating penetration and touch. In such situations, it has been found beneficial to initiate the dialogue with the drawings and then introduce the dolls as a demonstration aid. And although the drawings have not come under as much scrutiny as the dolls, some of the same arguments could be used for and against them.

The dolls and drawings are helpful not only to young children, but also older children and adolescents who may find it difficult to discuss the allegations. An interviewer needs to be aware of the opposing positions related to the use of the dolls, so he/she can utilize them as effectively and proficiently as possible.

The anatomically detailed dolls were introduced in the late 1970s, and since then there have been numerous discussions advocating and protesting their use (White, 1988; Freemant & Estrada-Mullany, 1988; White & Santilli, 1988; Boat & Everson, 1990 and 1994; & Lie & Inman, 1991; Elliott & O'Donohue, 1993; Goodman & Aman, 1990; American Professional Society on the Abuse of Children, 1990; Cohn, 1991; Yates & Terr, 1988; Kendall-Tackett, 1992; Bays, 1990; Whitcomb, 1992; Myers, 1992; Rainey, 1994A; Rainey, 1994B; and Faller, 1996).

Proponents state the dolls have the following benefits when they are used properly:

1. Toys are a means by which children express themselves. The dolls are child-oriented, thus children relate well to them.

2. The dolls can help decrease a child's anxiety. Dolls are a child's toy and reduce the formality and rigidity of the interviewer's office or room.

3. The dolls can reduce vocabulary problems. If a child is unable to articulate elements of the allegation, dolls can be used to demonstrate.

4. When a child has the vocabulary but is embarrassed, dolls can be used to show or demonstrate the activity.

Opponents' views of the dolls are:

1. The dolls are overly suggestive and will elicit sexual behaviors, responses, and fantasies in abused as well as nonabused children.

2. The sight of the dolls' genitalia provokes horror and alarm in children.

3. The dolls might contaminate the child's memory through the child's exposure to their genitalia.

4. No scientific evidence validates the use of the dolls.

5. The doll's genitalia are enlarged and not proportional with those of humans.

With such controversy, numerous studies have been conducted on the dolls. The majority have provided support for the use of the anatomically detailed dolls. Boat and Everson (1990) offered considerable data that the anatomically detailed dolls do not induce sexual play in young, nonabused children. Likewise, Cohn (1991) found that sexually abused children were more likely to engage in sexual behavior with the dolls than those children who were not abused. This study noted that many children who were indeed abused will not demonstrate the abuse on the dolls, and a small percentage of nonabused children will demonstrate sexual play.

Goodman and Aman (1990) found that the dolls do not influence a child to make a false report, even when the child is placed under conditions of intense suggestibility. Boat and Everson (1990) reported that the anatomically detailed dolls provide abused children with an "implicit permission as well as an easy vehicle for revealing their sexual knowledge." MacFarlane (1995) reported that abused children frequently avoid discussing sexual matters. Having these topics introduced by the interviewer's aids rather than the child helps the disclosure process and the effectiveness of the interview.

Bays (1990) examined seventeen adult male and seventeen adult female dolls and found the genitalia to be proportional or smaller than normal compared to humans.

The one consistent caveat regarding the tools is that the interviewer must be trained to use them. An interviewer using the dolls should also be familiar with the guidelines issued by the American Professional Society on the Abuse of Children, which provide research findings and recommendations for proper use (APSAC, 1990). Finally, the author feels it is important for the interviewer not to see the dolls and drawings as the "end all" to a child's allegation, but rather as another tool to enhance the investigative process.

The interviewer should decide ahead of time which tools are to be used and place them accordingly in the interview room. An interviewer leaving the interview room to get tools can seem to a child as if what he/she has to say is not important or the interviewer does not wish to listen anymore. Furthermore, if the child is hesitant to disclose alleged abuse, an interviewer's absence may provide that child with an opportunity to decide not to talk.

The tools should be available to the interviewer within the room but should not be displayed. Toys within easy reach of the child may divert him/her from talking and may lead to a power struggle if the child does not wish to leave the toys alone and talk with the interviewer. We often think that children need to be surrounded by toys to make them comfortable. Several play therapists (Axline, 1947; Schaefer & Reid, 1986; Garbarino, Stott, et al, 1989; Sandler, Kennedy, & Tyson, 1980) have discussed how toys are children's means of communication and voice. However, they can also be used by the child as a silencer or distraction. If a child wishes not to talk, he/she can very easily become engaged in play. If an interviewer has to take a toy from a child or loses the child's interest while trying to discuss alleged abuse, an unnecessary power struggle has been created.

It is beneficial to have the toys in brightly colored canvas bags or storage bins stored in a cupboard or on a shelf in the room. They are easily accessible if the interviewer deems them necessary.

One other aspect of creating the environment is determining what items a child can be offered. Opinions vary on whether to provide a child with refreshments or trinkets. In the intervention milieu, furnishing beverages is typical. Similarly, several interviewing environments provide a child with juice or a soda. Others maintain that if a child is thirsty, a cup of water will suffice. Akin to beverages other than water, some interviewers provide the child with a stuffed animal or another small trinket after the interview. This gesture is intended to comfort. Concern has been raised that providing beverages and gifts can be perceived as a form of bribery. The decision to furnish items and the potential ramifications must be thoroughly discussed with the multidisciplinary team. If beverages are to be provided, a team needs to decide not only the type of beverage, but also whether it will be offered before the interview or only after a child requests it. Furthermore, if a trinket will be provided to a child, an interviewer should not allude to the item the child will receive.

(I): "After we talk today I have a toy for you."

This type of comment is seen as a bribe.

A useful tool is the wireless "bug in the ear." Using a single interviewer rather than a team in the room has its limitations. The interviewer may not acquire all the data needed by the different disciplines. Even the most skilled interviewer, one who has done several hundred interviews, still may need assistance in remembering what to ask, or may need clarification of information. For this reason a communication device, a small speaker in the ear, a "bug in the ear," has been used. This provides a multidisciplinary inquiry without the "professional bombardment" of the child. The interviewer is connected with various parties. Professionals can stand behind a mirror or in a monitoring room if the interview is videotaped, and thus call in to clarify information.

Furthermore, using a device such as this allows the interviewer to focus on the child without having to take notes. However, if an interviewer decides to take notes, it is strongly encouraged that he/she takes them throughout the interview. If an interviewer only takes notes when a child discloses, a heightened emphasis is put on the sexual encounters rather than the child's being. Furthermore, taking notes tells the child that this is what the interviewer was looking for, and if the child has adopted a pleasing mode this can lead to problems in obtaining an accurate disclosure.

The proper selection of tools, their placement, and their correct use are essential. With a room equipped with the necessary tools for a productive interview, the multidisciplinary team needs to determine how the interview will be recorded.

REFERENCES:

American Professional Society on the Abuse of Children. (1990). *Guidelines for use of anatomical dolls during investigative interviews of children who may have been sexually abused.* Chicago: American Professional Society on the Abuse of Children.

Axline, V.(1947). *Play therapy.* New York: Ballatine Books.

Barker, P. (1990). *Clinical interviews with children and adolescents.* New York: W.W. Norton and Co.

Bays, J. (1990). Are the genitalia of the anatomical dolls distorted? *Child Abuse and Neglect, 14,* 171-175.

Boat, B., & Everson, M. (1990). Sexualized doll play among young children: Implications for the use of anatomical dolls in sexual abuse evaluations. *Journal of the American Academy of Child and Adolescent Psychiatry, 29,* 736-742.

Boat, B., & Everson, M. (1994). Putting the anatomical doll controversy in perspective: An examination of the major uses and criticisms of the dolls in child sexual abuse evaluations. *Child Abuse and Neglect, 18,* 113-130.

Britton, H., & O'Keefe, M.A. (1991). Use of non-anatomical dolls in the sexual abuse interviews. *Child Abuse and Neglect, 15,* 567-573.

Cage, R. (1991). Personal Communication.

Cohn D. (1991). Anatomical doll play of preschoolers referred for sexual abuse and those not referred. *Child Abuse and Neglect, 15,* 455-466.

Conte, J.R., Sorenson, E., Fogarty, L., & Dalla Rosa, J. (1991). Evaluating children's reports of sexual abuse: Results from a survey of professionals. *American Journal of Orthopsychiatry, 61,* 428-437.

Elliott, A., & O'Donohue, W. (1993). The use of sexually anatomically detailed dolls in the assessment of sexual abuse. *Clinical Psychology Review, 13,* 207-221.

Faller, K. (1996). Evaluating children suspected of having been sexually abused: *The APSAC Study Guides, 2.* Thousand Oaks, CA: Sage Publications.

Freemant, K.R., & Estrada-Mullany, T. (1988). Using dolls to interview child victims: Legal concerns and interview procedures. *Research in action, National Institute of Justice, 2.*

Garbarino, J., Stott, F., & the Faculty of the Eriksonian Institute. (1989). *What children can tell us.* San Francisco: Jossey-Bass Publishers.

Goodman, G., & Aman, C. (1990). Children's use of anatomically correct dolls to recount an event. *Child Development, 61,* 1859-1871.

Groth, N., & Stevenson, T. (1990). *Anatomical drawings for use in investigation and intervention of child sexual abuse.* Florida: Forensic Mental Health Associates.

Jones, D.P.H., & McQuiston, M. (1988). *Interviewing the sexually abused child.* London: Gaskell.

Kendall-Tackett, K. (1992). Beyond anatomical dolls: Professionals' use of other play therapy techniques. *Child Abuse and Neglect, 16,* 139-142.

Kendall-Tackett, K., & Watson, M. (1991). Factors that influence professionals' perceptions of behavioral indicators of child sexual abuse. *Journal of Interpersonal Violence, 6,* 385-395.

Lie, G., & Inman, A. (1991). The use of anatomical dolls as assessment and evidentiary tools. *Social Work,* 396-399.

MacFarlane, K. (1995). Presentation for Giarretto Institute five day advanced forensic interviewing training for investigations of child sexual abuse. San Jose, CA.

Mead, J.J., Balch, G.M., & Maggio, E. (1985). *Investigating child abuse, 18-42.* CA: C. Law and Company.

Myers, J.E.B. (1992). *Legal issues in child abuse and neglect.* Thousand Oaks, CA: Sage Publications.

National Network of Children's Advocacy Centers. (1994). *Best practices: A guidebook to establishing a children's advocacy center program.* Huntsville, AL: National Network of Children's Advocacy Centers.

Rainey, R. (1994A). *Current issues and controversies in child abuse cases.* VA: National Center for Prosecution of Child Abuse. American Prosecutor's Research Institute.

Rainey, R. (1994B). *Videotaping investigative interviews.* VA: National Center for Prosecution of Child Abuse. American Prosecutor's Research Institute.

Sandler, J., Kennedy, H., & Tyson, R. (1980). *The technique of child psychoanalysis, discussions with Anna Freud.* Cambridge, MA: Harvard Press.

Schaefer, C., & Reid, S. (1986). *Game play: Therapeutic use of childhood games.* New York: John Wiley & Sons.

Sorenson, T., & Snow, B. (1991). How children tell: The process of disclosure in child sexual abuse. *Child Welfare, 70,* 39.

Spaulding, W. (1987). *Interviewing child victims of sexual exploitation* (pp. 1-22). Washington, DC: National Center for Missing Children.

Steward, M. (1989). *The development of a model interview for young child victims of sexual abuse. A study of the National Center on Child Abuse and Neglect.* University of California, Davis: Department of Psychiatry.

Whitcomb, D. (1992). *When the victim is a child* (2nd ed.). Washington, DC: U.S. Department Of Justice.

White, S. (1988). Should investigatory use of anatomical dolls be defined by the courts? *Journal of Interpersonal Violence, 13,* 471-475.

White, S., & Santilli, G. (1988). A review of clinical practices and research data on anatomical dolls. *Journal of Interpersonal Violence, 3,* 437-439.

Yates, A., & Terr, L. (1988). Issue continued: Anatomically correct dolls - Should they be used as a basis for expert testimony? *Journal of the American Academy of Child and Adolescent Psychiatry, 27,* 387-388.

Chapter 8

AUDIOVISUAL RECORDING OF INTERVIEWS

Videotaping interviews is a controversial subject (Yuille,Hunter, Joffe, & Zaparniuk, 1993; Whitcomb, 1992; National Center on Child Abuse and Neglect, 1988; Berliner, 1992; Stern, 1992; Stephenson, 1992; Geller, 1993; Dallas Children's Advocacy Center, 1994; Myers, 1992; Faller, 1996). There are advantages and disadvantages to videotaping interviews. The decision whether to videotape should not be taken lightly. It should be a shared determination by all members of the multidisciplinary team. To reach an informed decision, the advantages and disadvantages of videotaping need be explored.

The advantages of videotaping are as follows:

1. It reduces the number of times and the number of people who have to question the child directly.

2. It provides a detailed record of what occurred in the interview. Having a video-taped interview demonstrates accountability not only of the interview process, but also the interviewer. Often an interviewer's credibility and style of questioning are challenged. Documenting what occurred, on videotape can make this challenge moot if the interviewer is skilled and conducts the interview professionally. If the interview is done professionally, the interviewer's credibility should not be in question. The classic question of "what do you have to hide?" can arise if the interview is not taped. Furthermore, not having a videotape does not guarantee that an interviewer's credibility and style will not be attacked. A common tactic of the defense in criminal prosecution is to question the interviewer's style rather than challenge the child. If the interviewer is accused leading the child, video documentation can illustrate that a forensically sound interview was conducted.

3. Similarly, being videotaped, or viewed by others, enhances one's skills. An interviewer can have his/her work critiqued by peers and supervisors, thus leading to advancement of skills.

4. It has been asserted that a videotaped interview will capture the child's emotions, facial and body movements, and expressions. Frequently, however, children have a flat or blunted affect during the interview.

5. Videotaped interviews can be a valuable tool in obtaining an alleged perpetrator's confession. Once a videotaped interview ends, the videotape becomes the prop-

erty of the law enforcement officer. Often, the mere mention of the child's video-taped disclosure results in a confession by the alleged perpetrator. In a few cases, portions of the tape are shared with the alleged perpetrator, resulting in a confession. As with decisions in all areas of a child abuse investigation, the decision to reveal the child's videotaped disclosure should not be made lightly. The professionals need to assess whether it would be of benefit in obtaining a confession, or whether the tape would assist the alleged perpetrator in his/her denial.

Furthermore, it must be remembered throughout a child abuse investigation that if the child has been abused, his/her life has consisted of repeated exposure and exploitation. The role of intervening professionals is to balance the child's needs with what is needed to make a case. This is not to say that children will be completely protected from all situations that might expose or exploit them, but careful evaluation should occur before acting.

6. Videotaped interviews may benefit the nonoffending parent. The parent is usually curious about the disclosure. The nonoffending parent wants to know whether his/her child was abused, and if so, what the details are. Sometimes, learning the details from the investigative team is not enough for the parent. And the parents should be discouraged from asking the child for specifics. The child may have great difficulty telling the nonoffending parent. The child may feel embarrassed, guilty, as though he/she hurt the parent by "participating" in the abuse. Furthermore, a child should not be put in the position of having to nurture and support a parent once the parent has learned the details. Constant questioning regarding the abuse keeps the abuse alive as a central part of the child's existence. As previously emphasized, one of the goals of investigative multidisciplinary interviews is to reduce the number of times a child must relay the details. By allowing the nonoffending parent to view the tape, this objective will be further facilitated.

In situations where the nonoffending parent does not believe the child and is denying that the abuse has occurred, viewing the videotape can be a powerful experience. It can transform a nonbelieving, nonoffending parent into a believer.

Either way, the child should be consulted before providing the nonoffending parent access to the tape. This is recommended for the child's empowerment, as well as to decrease the level of exploitation and betrayal. This does not imply that permission is requested, but rather the child is informed and his/her feelings are discussed. When videotaped children are informed about who will likely view the videotape, the nonoffending parent should not be included in that list as a potential viewer. For the nonoffending parent to then view the tape without the child's prior knowledge is a betrayal of the child by the system.

7. Similarly, the videotaped interview can be an asset to the child's treatment. The videotape can be viewed by the child's therapist to assist in the treatment. If a therapist has viewed the video prior to seeing the child for the initial session, the

therapist's questions can be more therapeutic: "How has the abuse affected you?" rather than, "So, tell me what happened?" This is not to insinuate that the details of the abuse should never be discussed in treatment, for there is a time and place for that during the child's recovery.

8. Videotapes can also be used to enhance the trial preparation process. The prosecutor, prior to meeting with the child witness, can review the tape and ascertain the developmental level and skills of the child, thus structuring their first meeting in a way that is beneficial to both. The videotape can also be used during the meeting with the child witness. Reviewing the tape together can be less threatening than a straightforward "I question you, you answer me" discussion. Furthermore, the tape can be reintroduced, reviewed, and stopped to clear up any inconsistencies and questions.

For the child, the videotape can be reviewed to refresh his or her recollection of the details. Often, the trial does not occur until many months after the initial interview. During that time, a child has entered treatment and begun to resolve issues. A review of the videotape may prove beneficial.

9. Frequently, videotaped interviews facilitate a guilty plea before trial. However, if the case does go to trial, a videotaped interview may be a beneficial piece of evidence. In some jurisdictions, it can be used in place of a child's testimony. However, this raises the issue of the Sixth Amendment and the defendant's right to face-to-face confrontation of the accuser. In lieu of replacing the child's testimony, a videotape can supplement the child's testimony.

10. Having a videotaped recording of the child's disclosure may decrease the likelihood he/she will recant.

11. The videotape may be used by expert witnesses in formulating an opinion.

Although the advantages of videotaping are numerous, disadvantages also exist.

1. It is known that disclosure is not a one time occurrence, but a process (Sorenson & Snow, 1991). Typically, a child is interviewed only once. Thus, the child's entire disclosure of the abuse will not be captured on tape.

2. The presence of the video camera may make the child nervous, thus deterring him/her from disclosing.

3. There can be technical difficulties with the audiovisual equipment. If the interview tape quality is poor and replete with technical glitches, it may encourage the defense to question the credibility of the entire investigation.

4. In the courtroom, the focus may be directed to the interviewer's credibility rather than the child's disclosure, thus nullifying the significance of the child's disclosure.

5. The question of a child's right to confidentiality may be raised. In no other type of investigation is an alleged victim routinely videotaped. Furthermore, there is minimal control over who may potentially view the tape.

If the use of a video camera is agreed upon, attention needs to be placed on positioning it unobtrusively. The child needs to be aware of its presence, although it does not need to stare the child in the face. It is important for the child to know that he/she is being recorded. There is great likelihood that the child will learn about the tape at some point in the process, and if the interviewer has not informed him/her of such, the interviewer has betrayed the child. Such betrayal contradicts the therapeutic nature of the interview.

The interviewer should briefly acknowledge the camera and its role. The interviewer should not ask the child's permission to videotape because the ability to comply with the child's negative response is not an option. Instead, the interviewer should nonchalantly introduce the camera and proceed with rapport building and assessment. (This will be discussed further in Chapter 10.) If a child presents him/herself as agitated by or fearful of the camera, the interviewer should briefly attend to the child's feelings and then provide distraction by engaging the child in dialogue or an activity.

Although just audiotaping is not as routinely used, it does occur (usually in field settings outside an established child interviewing room). When practiced, similar steps should be taken.

The decision to use audiovisual recording of an investigative interview should not be taken lightly. Once agreed to, the execution of the equipment should be done meticulously. Chronicaling the child's disclosure and the process by which it occurred is of the upmost importance.

REFERENCES:

Berliner, L. (1992). Should investigative interviews of children be videotaped? *Journal of Interpersonal Violence, 17,* 277-278.

Dallas Children's Advocacy Center. (1994). Position statement: *Videotaping investigative interviews of children.* Dallas, TX: Author.

Faller, K. (1996). Evaluating children suspected of having been sexually abused: *The APSAC Study Guides, 2.* Thousand Oaks, CA: Sage Publications.

Geller, W. (1993). *Videotaping interrogations and confessions.* Washington, DC: U.S. Department of Justice, Institute of Justice.

Myers, J.E.B. (1992). *Legal issues in child abuse and neglect.* Thousand Oaks, CA: Sage Publications.

National Clearing House on Child Abuse and Neglect. (1988). Symposium on interviewing children.

Sorenson, T., & Snow, B. (1991). How children tell: The process of disclosure in child sexual abuse. *Child Welfare, 70,* 3-15.

Stephenson, C. (1992). Videotaping and how it works well in San Diego. *Journal of Interpersonal Violence, 17,* 184-288.

Stern, P. (1992). Videotaping child interviews: A detriment to an accurate determination of guilt. *Journal of Interpersonal Violence, 17,* 278-284.

Whitcomb, D. (1992). *When the victim is a child* (2nd ed.). Washington, DC: U.S. Department Of Justice.

Yuille, J.C., Hunter, R., Joffe, R., & Zaparniuk, J. (1993). Interviewing children in sexual abuse cases. In G. Goodman, and B. Bottoms (Eds.), *Child victims, child witnesses: Understanding and improving testimony.* New York: Guilford Press.

Chapter 9

THE FIRST PHASES: PRE-INTERVIEW COORDINATION, ENGAGING THE CHILD, AND COMPETENCY ASSESSMENT

Before conducting the interview, a multidisciplinary staffing of the case should occur. It is helpful to schedule this meeting immediately before the interview. During this brief meeting, the case is discussed. This allows the interviewer to learn key information regarding the child and the allegations, such as the alleged acts, the alleged perpetrator, family members' names, prior disclosures, witnesses, the nature of the disclosure, etc. It is important to note that the alleged perpetrator's name should not be used in the interview until the child has introduced it. It is important to know prior to the interview who the key people are so that as discussion evolves in the interview, the interviewer is aware of who these individuals may be and who has been ommitted from discussion.

In a comprehensive-collaborative child abuse investigation, the investigative team should complete the following steps before the interviewer meets the child:

1. Contact the referral source to learn the specific allegations and corroborating information.

2. Screen child welfare, law enforcement, Juvenile/Family Court and probation records for previous referrals and present action being taken.

3. If appropriate, contact the nonoffending parent to gather information regarding the child's behavior and information pertaining to the presenting problem. This step should be approached cautiously. It is not always known at the onset of the investigation whether the nonoffending parent is allied with the child, or is even a nonoffending parent. Thus, information from the nonoffending parent can either be gathered prior to the investigative interview or while the child is being interviewed.

4. Either prior to or within 72 hours of the child's interview, collateral sources in the child's life should be contacted. Typically they include a school or day care

teacher, physician, and intervening social service agencies and children's organizations.

Having the above information before the interview can assist the interviewer avoid unintentionally leading questions.

However, it should be cautioned that if an interviewer becomes too focused on the initial allegation, he/she may become biased and leave out the exploration of alternative hypotheses and realities.

Have several plans of action prior to being caught up in the interview. If the interviewer has several options and several routes available, when a roadblock occurs the interviewer will not be stalled, but rather can proceed in another direction. Knowing specific information about the child's life, his or her alleged abusive and nonabusive activities, and the key individuals in his/her life can assist an interviewer in directly questioning a child.

For example a child alleged he was abused by his brother's friend at the doctor's office. In an initial phase of the interview, the child discussed his life in general. Later, following the normal course of the interview, the child had not spontaneously disclosed the alleged abuse. Thus, the interviewer started to talk about family members and family members' friends. When this did not prove beneficial, the interviewer took another route: Who are the different professionals we see in our life? We see teachers, we see dentists and we see doctors. This directed dialogue resulted in the disclosure of the alleged abuse. Had the interviewer not been prepared upon initial discussion of family members and friends, he or she may have prematurely curtailed the interview.

Once the information is gathered, it is time to meet the child.

The current, accepted method of investigative interviewing has three stages: rapport building, information gathering, and closure. Each stage complements the next, and all stages have equal importance in a comprehensive, forensically and therapeutically sound investigation.

The rapport-building portion of the interview gives the child a chance to become acclimated to the interviewer and the interview setting. It also allows the interviewer to assess the child and lay the framework of the interview. For most children, entering the interview environment can be unsettling. This is not a familiar playing field. Allowing the child time to become better acquainted with the room and the interviewer can be advantageous. Research has found that children who engage in more rapport building with the interviewer had fewer errors than those who did not. (Matthews & Saywitz, 1992). Furthermore, spending time with the child and getting to know non-abuse-related information about the child allows him/her to retain the position of primary importance. The alleged abuse is secondary. Moreover, Sternberg, Lamb, Hershkowitz, Orbach, Hovav, and Esplin, (1996) found that a well-conducted rapport phase reduced the amount of direct questioning needed later in the interview.

Besides assisting the child, the rapport-building phase facilitates the developmental assessment. During benign dialogue,the interviewer should be ascertaining the child's speech and verbal ability, the child's skill at answering questions, his/her ability to understand prepositions, time and core concepts, and his/her nonverbal communication, i.e., breathing pattern and eye contact.

This phase of the interview also sets the stage for the pattern of the interviewer asking a question and the child furnishing an answer. The interviewer can also use this time to decrease a child's existing or potential anxiety by acknowledging the child's feelings and giving the child some sense of control.

Rapport building begins in the waiting room. Although waiting room dialogue should be brief, it is crucial. An interviewer should immediately get to the child's level and introduce him/herself.

(I): "Hi, Bobby. I'm _____. It's nice to meet you. Is this your mom/dad?"

Once the interviewer meets the child, the parent(s) should be attended to. If it is discovered during the pre-interview preparation that the parent is supportive, the following question could be asked:

(I): "I'm glad Bobby is here today to talk with me. Is it all right for us to talk about anything?"

If there is the slightest chance that a parent will respond negatively to this question, it should not be posed. Rather, a simple request of permission for the child to join the interviewer in the interviewing room is sufficient. No matter which question is asked, it is imperative that the child listen to the dialogue.

Another dilemma regarding the parent that may arise is parental contamination. This occurs when a parent has naively, not maliciously, promised the child a treat if the child talks with the interviewer.

(C): "My daddy said he'd take me for ice cream once I talked with you."

(I): "Okay, that's something between you and your daddy.

All that I expect of you is for you and me to talk about the truth."

An example of parental contamination is when a parent warns the child of the negative ramifications of disclosing, or when the child has overheard the parents' discussing the ramifications.

(C): "My mommy said that I'll have to live somewhere else. My daddy will go away and I'll have to go to court."

(I): "Tell me about your concerns/worries" or "Well, I can't tell you what will happen because I don't know about your situation, but let's start at the beginning, and let's see if we can sort things out."

Just as parents have the power to contaminate, interviewers also have inherent power in the interviewing room. Immediately upon entering the room, the interviewer should impart some of his/her power. Simple questions can facilitate this.

"Where should I sit?"

"What name do you like to go by?"

If a child appears hesitant or if the interviewer assesses that the direct format of sitting down, making eye contact, and answering questions will be difficult, the child should promptly be engaged in an activity. A hesitant child should not have attention drawn to his/her avoidant behavior.

(I): "Are you going to talk with me today?"

This type of statement can make the child even less inclined to disclose. Engaging the child will be more productive. A reliable exercise is drawing (Burgess & Hartman, 1993; and Farley, 1987; Saywitz et al, 1992). This activity provides a distraction from eye-to-eye contact while permitting dialogue to occur. It can also be entered into jointly by the child and the interviewer.

If a hesitant child is reluctant to draw and resistant to talking, the interviewer could begin coloring him/herself and then attempt to engage the child by asking, "Where should the flowers/tree/eyes/etc., go?"

Once settled or if not already addressed, the interviewer should briefly acquaint the child with the audiovisual equipment.

(I): "Mary, do you see that [pointing to camera] over there? Do you know what it is?...That's right it's a camera. Have you ever seen one before?...I have one here because I talk with lots of kids and some of those kids need help, and for those kids since we taped our talk they don't have to tell a lot of people. It's not like 'America's Funniest Home Videos,' it's not shown on T.V. It's only shown to people who can help those kids."

This dialogue accomplishes several things. First, it introduces the camera. As discussed, a child needs to know that he/she is being videotaped. It also informs the child that the videotape will be seen by other professionals. Also, if the child has been abused, the statement may imply that the child is not alone, there are other children who have been abused. Lastly, and most significantly, never in this dialogue is it implied that the child has a problem.

The "bug in the ear" communication device also deserves an introduction.

(I): "See this thing? Have you ever seen one of these before?...Most people haven't! This is in my ear so if anyone needs to get ahold of me, they can call in on this instead of knocking on the door. I want to talk with you, and I don't want someone coming in and bothering us."

Most notable in both these descriptions is the omission of asking the child's permission. Experience shows that a brief, nonchalant introduction followed immediately by dialogue related to the child takes the emphasis off the equipment. For a child who blatantly shows distress, an interviewer should take the time to process his/her feelings, and then proceed with rapport-building questions.

The next step in this phase is to become acquainted with the child and to introduce the concept of asking questions. The questions should be nonthreatening and should engage the child.

Children are used to routine questions to which the questioner does not listen to the response. Rapport-building questions should break the ice and convey the interviewer's attentiveness. Although they may appear to be casual, they are not, for they address the child as a child, not a victim, and they set the stage for the "I ask a question, you answer" format of the interview. An interviewer should have a standard set of several questions, phrased age specifically, from which he/she can easily draw.

"What do you do for a living?"

"Do you have a pet? What's his/her name? What does he/she look like? What kind of things do you do with him/her?"

"What's your favorite game?...How do you play that?"

"What do you like to eat?"

"Do you smoke?"

"Who lives in your house?"

"Do you drive?"

These questions allow the child to share part of his/her life with the interviewer. They also allow the child to be the guide and to educate the interviewer, which will be expected of the child if a disclosure is made.

Following the initial dialogue and introductions, an interviewer can choose to assess the child's understanding of prepositions or the child's competency for being truthful. Both items need to be addressed, an interviewer needs to determine in which sequence he/she wishes to address them. For older children, the task of showing knowledge of prepositions is done though their rapport building dialogue.

It is recommended that competency assessment occur before the information-gathering phase of the interview. If the child has disclosed and the interviewer then assesses competency, the interviewer's message may convey mistrust of the child's previous statement.

Competency standards vary from state to state. In general, the courts have set forth the following areas to measure a child's competency to testify: capacity for truthfulness, mental capacity at the time of the event to accurately gather impressions of it, sufficient memory retention, and the ability to communicate (Whitcomb, 1992). Experience has found that three elements need to be addressed. First, the child must demonstrate that he/she knows the difference between the truth and a lie. Next, that he/she knows the consequences of telling a lie; and lastly, he/she accepts the obligation to tell the truth.

Bussey (1992) found that by age 4, children understand the difference between the truth and a lie and are aware that it is bad or wrong to tell a lie. Matthews and Saywitz (1992), however, discovered that most children, especially younger ones, do not understand the word "difference". Similarly, Lyon (1996) found that children, by age 5, have a good understanding of the definition of truth and lie and the related ethics.

However, Lyon and Saywitz's research (1996) provides the interviewer with valuable information regarding how younger children should be questioned regarding competency. They divided the competency question into three tasks: the difference task, defining the difference between a truth and a lie; the definition task, explaining what it means to tell the truth; and the identification task, being able to identify statements as truthful or a lie. They found that by age 7, a child can define, tell the difference, and identify. However, children younger than 7 are less competent at satisfactorily completing the definition and the difference tests, but are proficient with the identification task. Also noteworthy, Lyon and Saywitz 1996 found that children younger than 4 appear to be reluctant to talk about lies and do better when discussing lies regarding a third person, not themselves or the interviewer. This is invaluable information, which correctly throws the responsibility back on the interviewer to ask questions in the right manner.

For younger children, the competency examination should begin like this:

(I): "One of the things I talk with kids about is the truth? If I said you were a boy, would that be true?"

(C): "Yes."

(I): "It would be true. Because you are a boy. The truth is something that really is or really happened."

The interviewer would then proceed with two or three other examples. Different competency samples include:

Is there a cat in the picture?

Is the boy (in the picture) wearing a dress/shoes?

Does the girl have a ponytail?

Is there a window in this room?

Is there a horse sitting next to me?

If I said your name was Mortimer?

If I said you were a boy?

Then the interviewer should introduce the concept of lie.

(I): "If I said you were a girl. What would that be?"

(C): "A fib."

(I): "It would be a fib, or sometimes I call it a lie too. A lie is something that isn't true. It's made up."

And again, the child would be questioned on two other items. It is important to break these concepts down for a clearer understanding. Also, the truth should be addressed first. It is what is being emphasized in the investigation. Also, with older children, if the concept of lie is introduced first, they may beleive that the interviewer has a pre-conceived notion that he/she is a liar.

Another tactic for assisting the child in identifying truths and lies is using a technique created by Lyon, Saywitz, and Durato (1996). Illustration cards that show an object such as an apple accompanied by two stick figures are used. One stick figure has a thought bubble over its head with a picture of an apple; the other has a thought bubble with a picture of a banana. The interviewer asks the child to name the object not in a thought bubble, then asks the child to identify who is being truthful and who is not.

Cage (1991) recommends using a color and/or animal chart for competency review. These charts are easily made with colored cardboard with pictures of animals and colors adhered to it. Experience has shown that these boards are beneficial for assessing developmental issues rather than for competency. Colors are better known by school- age children, rather than younger children, as the following case illustrates:

(I): "Do you know all your colors?"

(C): "Yeah."

(I): (Showing green circle) "What color is this?"

(C): "Blue."

(I): (Showing the red circle) "What color is this?"

(C): "Green."

An interviewer cannot guarantee that a young child correctly knows colors. An interviewer may interview a child who is colorblind. Unfortunately, in both cases, a child could be considered as non-credible when indeed the child could "pass" the examination. However, if colors are used in the developmental assessment, an interviewer should see if the child can identify red, yellow, and white. Since these colors are most closely associated with evidence and details regarding child sexual abuse.

With children older than 7, this phase of the interview has them define and illustrate the difference between a truth and lie. Some children can provide information without assistance.

(I): "One of the things that I talk with kids about is truths. Can you tell me what a truth is, what it means to tell the truth?"

(C): "A truth is what really happens."

(I): "Good. How about a lie, what does that mean?"

(C): "Something that didn't."

(I): Give me an example of a truth."

(C): "I am a girl."

(I): "Okay, how about another?"

(C): "I have red hair."

(I): "Okay, and an example of a lie?"

(C): "I am a boy."

(I): "Okay, and how about one more?"

(C): "It's snowing today.

(I): "Good. Can you give me an example of a boy telling a lie?"

(C): "If he stole a candy bar and when his mom asked him if he did, he says, 'No.'"

However, other children need assistance.

(I): "One of the things that I talk with kids about is truth. Can you tell me what a truth is? What it means to tell the truth?"

(C): "A truth is what's true."

(I): "It's kind of a tough thing to put into words. Let me help. If I said it was sunny today would that be true?"

(C): "Yeah."

(I): "That's correct; it is true, because it is sunny. A truth is something that is, that really happens or is happening. Okay, your turn. Give me an example of something that is true."

(C): "I am a girl."

(I): "Okay, how about another truthful statement?"

(C): "I have red hair."

(I): "Okay, give me an example of something that is a lie?"

(C): "Um, I don't know."

(I): "Okay, I'll give an example first. An example of a lie would be my saying it is raining outside today. How come that would be a lie?"

(C): "Because it isn't."

(I): "Right, a lie is something that really isn't. Your turn! Give me an example of a lie."

(C): "I like spinach."

(I): "How come that would be a lie?"

(C): "Because I hate it!"

(I): "Okay! How about another example of something that is a lie?"

(C): "I am a boy."

(I): "Okay. Can you give me an example of a boy telling a lie?"

(C): "Huh?"

(I): "Give me an example of someone purposely telling a lie. Someone who is trying to pull one over on someone else?"

(C): "Um..."

(I): "It's sometimes tough to come up with examples. Let me help. If a boy stole a candy bar and when his mom asked him if he did, he says, 'No'. Is he telling the truth or is he lying?"

(C): "He's lying, because he did steal it."

(I): "Right, now you give me an example."

In this sequence, the interviewer must provide examples first. If this occurs, it is important for the child to clarify his/her responses. Otherwise, it can appear as though the child was fortunate to get the correct answers, but it is not clear if the child understands the difference and definition of truths and lies. As with younger children, it is beneficial to get the older child to relay a few examples of a truth and a lie. Also an older child should provide an example to portray an understanding of deception.

It is important that the child does not define truths and lies as real versus pretend or right versus wrong. Either of these dichotomies is not a truth versus a lie. A child can define truth as something that really happened, though.

The second step of the competency examination is evaluating the child's comprehension of the consequences for not telling the truth. A child should be asked this in a third-person format rather than directly about him/herself.

(I): "What happens to a (gender opposite of the child's) if he/she tells a lie?"

Quite possibly, if the interviewer phrased this question as, "What happens to you..." the child would assume that either he/she has done something wrong or the interviewer already does not believe him/her, both of which could be detrimental to a potential disclosure.

Finally, the child needs to enter into an agreement to tell the truth:

(I): "Can we agree to only talk about the truth in here today?" or,

(I): "We only tell truths in here. Can you and I agree to tell the truth?"

Both of the examples illustrate an important point. The agreement is for both the child and the interviewer to tell the truth.

Once the three areas of competency have been addressed, it is a logical time to incorporate the other options for responding to a question. These options include "I don't know," "I don't understand," and "I don't remember." An interviewer should also have available in his/her repertoire "I don't want to talk about it." This is usually brought up when a child repeatedly uses one of the above escapes.

(I): "If I ask you a question which you don't know the answer to, that's okay. Just tell me, 'I don't know.' I won't be mad. It's real important that we don't guess at answers."

(I): "Sometimes I can ask some strange questions and if what I ask you doesn't make sense, just tell me, 'I don't understand.' I'll try again!"

(I): "If you can't remember something, that's okay. I would like you to tell me you can't remember. I don't want you to try and make something up." (As a side note, if a child frequently uses this during an interview, the interviewer might want to ask the child, "What would happen if you did remember?")

(I): "Do you not remember or do you not want to talk about it?"

A final instruction is for the interviewer to give the child permission to correct him/her.

(I): "I sometimes get things wrong, and if I do please let me know. Because it's important for both you and me to talk about the truth."

Either during or following this stage of the interview, the interviewer should test the child for suggestibility. This is done by the interviewer making erroneous statements regarding the color of crayons, the child's name, the weather, etc.

The competency examination should be addressed in a matter-of-fact manner. It should not have a heightened emphasis. It should appear to a child that this is as routine as asking about the weather forecast. This examination can be done thoroughly in a brief amount of time. However, there are a few areas that can create difficulty. Children who relay that they have lied before and children who start teasing the interviewer and making a mockery of the competency examination can sabotage their credibility.

> (I): "One of the things that I talk with kids about is truth and lies. Can you tell me what a truth is, what it means to tell the truth?"

> (C): "I lied to my mom."

> (I): "What do you mean?"

> (C): "I didn't tell her everything about a party I went to."

> (I): (Following the gathering of the details related to the party and the child's reasoning for not telling) "Okay, so you didn't tell her everything. However, it's real important that you and I talk about everything and tell the truth in here. Okay?"

> (C): "Sure."

> (I): "Good. Okay, can you tell me what it means to tell the truth?"

The interviewer needed to address the child's statement, and then revisit the child's credibility and willingness to tell the truth. In situations where a child initiates a disclosure of abuse before or during the competency phase, it is prudent for the interviewer to follow the child's lead and obtain a complete disclosure. After the abuse details have been gathered, the interviewer should reintroduce the competency examination.

> (I): "You know this whole discussion began when I was asking you questions about truths and lies. I need to go back and ask you about them. This is something I have to do every time I talk with someone."

Periodically, younger children will get into a game with the interviewer regarding true and false statements. An interviewer needs to swiftly attend to the child's joking.

> (I): "Do I have a dog on my lap?"

> (C): "Yep!"

> (I): "I do, where is he?"

> (C): "Um...I was joking."

(I): "Okay. I know it's fun to joke, but in here you and I need to tell the truth."

Here the interviewer has addressed the child's erroneous statement without admonishing the child. The interviewer has also redirected the interview back to the importance of both the child and the interviewer sharing correct information.

In cases where a child is performing poorly on the competency examination, it is important for the interviewer not to dwell on getting the "correct" answers. If too much time and energy are focused in this area, the child may be exhausted by the time the interview has progressed into the information-gathering portion.

Some children can give an accurate description of what has occurred but have difficulty in answering questions regarding truths and lies. So the interviewer needs to proceed to information gathering.

REFERENCES:

Burgess, A., & Hartman, C. (1993). Children's drawings. *Child Abuse and Neglect, 17,* 161-168.

Bussey, K. (1992). *Children's lying and truthfulness: Implications for children's testimony.* In S.J. Ceci, M.D. Leichtman, & M. Putnick (Eds.), Cognitive and social factors in early deception (pp. 89-109). Englewood Cliffs, New Jersey: Lawrence Erlbaum Associates.

Cage, R. (1991). Personal communication.

Durato, J. (1996). *New approaches to competency examinations. Advanced forensic interview training.* CA: Children's Institute International.

Farley, R. (1987). *Drawing interviews: An alternative to the anatomical dolls.* Police Chief, International Association of Chiefs of Police, April.

Lyon, T. (1996). Assessing children's competence to take the oath: Research and recommendations. *The APSAC Advisor, 9,* 1-7.

Matthews, E., & Saywitz, K. (1992). Child victim witness manual. *California Center for Judicial Education and Research Journal, 12,* 5-81.

Saywitz, K., Geiselman, R., & Bornstein, G. (1992). Effects of cognitive interviewing and practice on children's recall performance. *Journal of Applied Psychology, 77,* 744-756.

Sternberg, K., Lamb, M., Hershkowitz, I., Orbach, Y., Hovav, M., & Esplin, P. (1996). Effects of introductory style on children's accounts of sexual abuse. In A. Warren, C. Woodall, J. Hunt, & N. Perry. It sounds good in theory but... Do investigative interviews follow guidelines based on memory research? *Child Maltreatment, 1,* 231-245.

Whitcomb, D. (1992). *When the victim is a child* (2nd ed.). Washington, DC: U.S. Department of Justice.

Chapter 10

INFORMATION THAT NEEDS TO BE GATHERED

The child is the informant. An interviewer initially should listen to the child's complete narrative, without interruption. Then, the interviewer should attempt to gather the following information. This information should be acquired for each alleged incident of abuse that is discussed.

1. Identity and description of the alleged perpetrator(s).

2. Acts that occurred in the alleged abuse.

3. Number of times and the differences associated with each alleged incident of abuse.

4. Conversations and the style of coercion that occurred before, during, and/or following the alleged abuse.

5. Sensory details.

6. Instrument(s) used in or related to the alleged abuse.

7. Possibility of the use of pornography.

8. Possibility of drug and/or alcohol involvement.

9. Scenario leading to the alleged abuse.

10. Possibility of physical injury (perceived or verified).

11. Where the alleged abuse occurred.

12. Time of day, date, and year of the alleged abuse.

13. Whereabouts of others at the location of the alleged abuse.

14. Possibility of someone observing the alleged abuse.

15. Name(s) of individual(s) to whom the child reported the alleged abuse.

16. Other possible victims of the alleged perpetrator.

17. Other children who have contact with the alleged perpetrator.

18. Motivation for the disclosure.

Using a team approach for each interview, complemented with the "bug in the ear," the interviewer does not have to memorize these questions. Rather, the team can maintain a checklist of those questions that have been asked and prompt the interviewer on those omitted. However, it is the interviewer's responsibility to ask for the information in an appropriate manner. A nonexclusive list of specific questions employed to acquire and clarify information follows. For simplicity, pronouns are used. In an investigative interview, the pronouns would be replaced by specific references used by the child.

1. Identity and description of the alleged perpetrator(s).

What was his/her name (first and last)?

How did you meet/know him/her?

Where does he/she live?

Physical description: start at head work down to toes,:

What color was his/her hair?

How long was it?

What color were his/her eyes?

Any unusual marks on his/her (specific body area)?

2. Acts that occurred in the alleged abuse.

What did he/she do then?

What happened next?

What else?

What did he/she have you do?

He/she touched you on your vagina, what else?

(repeat child's statement). What happened next?

3. Number of times and the differences associated with each alleged incident of abuse.

How often would this happen?

Did it happen one time or a bunch of times?

Did it happen one day/night or a lot of days/nights?

Did it happen in the same room each time?

Name all the places this happened.

(Using the child's drawing of the crime scene) Each time, in

the bedroom, was it the same? What else happened in this room?

4. Conversations and the style of coercion that occurred before, during, and/or following the alleged abuse.

What did he/she say to you?

Did he/she say anything to you?

Did you say anything?

Did he/she say anything to you about telling someone about what happened?

What was it that made you stay there?

What did he/she say to you about what he/she would do?

What did he/she say about talking about what he/she did?

What kept you in the room?

What made you think you had to stay there?

What made you think that you couldn't get away?

What did you think would happen if you tried to leave the room?...What made

you think that?

Where were his/her hands?

5. Sensory details.

How did his penis look?

Which way did it point? Straight out? Pointed to the ground?

Was it firm or wobbly?

Did he/she make any sounds/noises?

When he/she finished? What did you notice?

When he was finished, was it wet or dry between your legs?

Do you know where the wet came from?

What can you tell me about the room?

What can you tell me about his/her movements?

Using your senses (eyes, nose, mouth, ears), what happened?

What did it taste like? etc.

6. Instrument(s) used in or related to the alleged abuse.

What did he/she touch you with?...What else?

What did he/she have you touch him with?

Did he/she use anything else?

7. Possibility of the use of pornography.

Any cameras, books, videotaping equipment, movies, etc., in the house?

Ever used/seen by _____?

Had you ever seen anyone else doing something like what you and he/she did?

Did he/she show you anything (pictures, magazines, videos)?

Did he/she take any pictures?

Did he/she make any movies?

8. Possibility of drug and/or alcohol involvement.

   Did you drink anything? Eat anything?

   How did you feel after eating/drinking _____?

   Did you feel sleepy?

   Did you see anybody smoking? What were they smoking?

9. Scenario leading to the alleged abuse

   How did you get into the bedroom? Where were you before that?

   How did he/she get into the house?

   What were you doing? What was he/she doing?

   Where were your clothes? Where were his/her clothes?

   How did your clothes get there?

   How did you end up alone with him/her?

10. Possibility of physical injury (perceived or verified).

    What happened to your body?

    How did it feel (to your body)?

11. Where the alleged abuse occurred

    Where were you when he/she touched you?

    Did this happen anywhere else?

    Whose bedroom, in whose house?

    What is the address of the house?

    I've never been there, what does the house look like?

    I've never been there, what did the room look like?

12. Time of day, date, and year of the alleged abuse.

    Was it light/dark outside?

    What type of clothing were you wearing?

    What time of year was it? (Spring, Summer, etc.)

    What grade were you in? Who was your teacher?

    Were you in school during the day? (Avoid using the word vacation for young

    children. They are always on vacation!)

    Did something special happen around this time (i.e. birthday, holiday)?

13. Whereabouts of others at the location of the alleged abuse.

    Who else was in the house? Where were they?

    Where was your mom/dad/brother/etc.?

14. Possibility of someone observing the alleged abuse.

    Was anyone else in the room?

    Did anyone else see what happened?

    Could anyone else have seen/known?

15. Name(s) of individual(s) to whom the child reported the alleged abuse.

    Who else might have known about this?

    Whom did you tell?

    What did he/she do about it?

16. Other possible victims of the alleged perpetrator.

    Did you see him/her do anything to anyone else?

    Who else did he/she do this to?

    How do you know that?

17. Other children who have contact with the alleged perpetrator.

    Who does he/she hang out with?

    What kids play/visit with him/her?

    Who else do you think he/she may have been with/done this with?

18. Motivation for the disclosure.

    Tell me what happened right before you decided to tell.

    How come you are able to tell now?

    What made it possible for you to tell?

    How did you feel about him/her then/now?

Another area which interviewer's may need to address is non-consensual adolescent sexual activity. Possible questions for this topic include:

You said people thought you caused this, how come?

How did you feel about him/her before this happened?

How did you feel about him/her after?

How did you feel about the attention he/she gave you?

How did you feel about his/her actions?

Three strategies to assist in the questioning are drawings, a time line, and the cognitive interview approach.

The first strategy, which is beneficial not only to the interviewer but also to the child, is to have the child draw a picture of the alleged crime scene. This will help the child to relay details and it provides the interviewer with a visual cue to facilitate questions. This technique is also advantageous when multiple venues for the alleged abuse exist. Simply, once a child identifies all of the locations where the alleged abuse took place, he/she should draw a separate picture for each location.

(I): "Okay Bobby, we were just talking about the time in the bedroom [pushing the bedroom picture aside and bringing the bathroom picture to the center of the table], now let's talk about the time in the bathroom."

The second strategy is beneficial in long-term, multi-incident cases. The child is asked to complete a time line of all the incidents of sexual activity. Once the basics of each incident are written down, the interviewer can guide the child through a detailed recounting of each. This technique helps the child focus on one situation at a time.

Another option for gathering the details of the alleged abuse advocated by Saywitz, Geiselman, and Bornstein (1992) is a cognitive interview. In this approach, a child is asked to reconstruct the circumstances from free recall. The interviewer asks the child to report everything from the beginning, through the middle to the end of the event. The child is encouraged to provide facts and feelings regarding the alleged abuse. After the initial disclosure, the interviewer asks the child to relay the event backwards and from a third person's perspective, i.e., through a stuffed animal's eyes. Then the interviewer asks questions such as the alleged perpetrator's appearance, conversations that occurred, etc. This type of interview is most effective with children older than 7 and when the child has practiced the technique with a benign event. It is a good technique to use in extended forensic assessments.

These questions and strategies can directly assist the multidisciplinary team with the criminal justice needs as well as the child protection needs. Both are of equal importance. Knowing what to ask is as important as knowing how to ask.

REFERENCES:

Saywitz, K., Geiselman, R., & Bornstein, G. (1992). Effects of cognitive interviewing and practice on children's recall performance. *Journal of Applied Psychology, 77,* 744-756.

Chapter 11

INFORMATION GATHERING

The primary objective of the interview is to gather information that will render a plausible hypothesis for the referral. The emphasis is on gathering the truth. If the allegation of abuse is valid, the intent of this phase of the interview is to have the child produce a spontaneous disclosure and to collect as many details regarding the alleged abuse as possible. Likewise, if the allegation is fictitious, the intent of this phase is to gather information that corroborates that conclusion.

The information-gathering portion of the interview models Faller's funnel approach to questioning (1990). The discussion should begin with a broad approach, followed by directed or refined discussion. An interviewer should commence the dialogue with a general question related to the child's presence and a reasonable explanation. If this does not facilitate disclosure, then dialogue related to feelings should be introduced, followed then, in cases of alleged incest, by a discussion of family members, then a discussion of types of touching. Finally, the conversation should focus on the particulars of the child's life.

If a child has been abused, at the point at which he/she provides a disclosure, the interview should be shifted away from the above sequence, and the interviewer should attend to gathering the particulars of the child's report, as detailed in Chapter 10.

The interviewer should begin to focus the interview on information gathering. The interviewer should acquaint the child with his/her role. Two standard dialogues are:

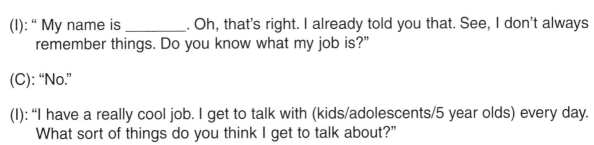

(I): " My name is _____. Oh, that's right. I already told you that. See, I don't always remember things. Do you know what my job is?"

(C): "No."

(I): "I have a really cool job. I get to talk with (kids/adolescents/5 year olds) every day. What sort of things do you think I get to talk about?"

Or:

(I): "Do you know what a social worker/detective does?"

(C): "No."

(I): "Most kids don't. It's kind of a strange job, but it's a cool job..."

In the above dialogue, if a child says he/she understands the interviewer's job, the interviewer should listen to the child's explanation, and respond accordingly:

> (I): "Boy, that's a pretty good explanation. I do that, plus I get to talk with..."

This dialogue projects a wealth of information. First, it relays that the interviewer thinks his/her job is enjoyable. The statement of it being "cool" portrays a sense of "I am okay with this topic" to a child who has been abused and knows why he/she is present. It conveys a sense of security. Furthermore, the statement about having spoken with numerous children conveys the interviewer's experience and may allow the child, if abused, to realize that he/she is not the only one with this problem.

This dialogue begins with the interviewer reintroducing him/herself. This is beneficial on two levels. First, it reminds the child of the interviewer's name. Frequently, a child has not remembered the interviewer's name, and reacquainting the child with it can create a sense of familiarity in the interview setting. It is not recommended to say to the child, "Do you remember my name?"

If he/she has forgotten it, this may embarrass the child. However, if the words come out of the interviewer's mouth, they can be quickly corrected by simply and immediately following the question with:

> (I): "Oops, that's right, I already told you my name was _____. See, I forget things some-times."

Secondly, it shows the child that the interviewer can make mistakes and self-correct. It implies that saying, "I don't know," or, "I don't remember," is acceptable.

If a child's explanation for being present with the interviewer does not generate a disclosure, the interviewer should continue to direct the interview. The conversation should then center on dialogue regarding feelings one might have. A discusssion of feelings provides an avenue that can generate a disclosure, which is not as direct as initially talking about touching.

> (I): "One of the things that I talk with kids about is feelings. What feelings do you know?"

If the child responds affirmatively, the interviewer should follow the child's lead. Many children will respond negatively, which is understandable because describing feelings is difficult enough for adults, let alone for a child who may have experienced no validation of feelings or even been allowed to express them. If this occurs, the following dialogue is recommended:

> (I): Most kids I talk to can't answer that question. They know what feelings are, but it's hard to put them into words. Let's see if I can help. One feeling I talk about is happy. What makes you happy?"

Once the child has responded to the question, the interviewer should ask, "What else makes you _____?" and "Who else makes you _____?" If a disclosure results from the specific feeling dialogue, the interviewer should proceed to gather the abuse details. However, if it does not, the interviewer should complete the discussion of at least the four basic feelings: happy, mad, sad, and scared. Once they have been discussed, an interviewer should ask the child to supply any additional feelings:

> (I): So we've discussed happy, mad, sad, and scared, what are some other feelings you have?"

The logic for this question is related to interpretation and perception. What one person might describe as fun could be horrifying to another, i.e., a haunted house visit or a roller-coaster ride. It is very important for an interviewer to avoid placing his/her interpretation on the child's experiences. An opportunity for disclosure can be lost if an interviewer assumes what the child feels.

> (I): (to an adolescent incest victim) "Has anything ever made you uncomfortable?"

> (C): "No."

> (I): "Has there been something that concerns or worries you?"

> (C): "No."

Later in the interview, during the touching dialogue, the adolescent disclosed. The interviewer then appropriatelyasked a feeling question:

> (I): "How did it make you feel?"

> (C): "I was embarrassed."

The child was embarrassed, not uncomfortable or worried. This shows how the interviewer's assumptions of what feelings would be related stalled a disclosure during the feeling question phase. Among the phrases that should be avoided are:

"That sounds (fun, scary, etc.)"

"That probably hurt."

"I bet that was uncomfortable, how was it?"

Phrases such as:

"I can guess what it felt like, but how was it for you?"

are better.

An interviewer should ask the child to provide an example of a time when he/she felt the feeling. However, if the child is unable to, the interviewer should have a few standard answers. These answers should be reviewed by the multidisciplinary team before the interview to ensure that the typically benign examples will not contaminate the current investigation. A sample of standard examples include:

Happy: playing with my friends, getting a gift, a sunny day

Sad: loosing my favorite toy, not getting dessert, a toy breaks, someone hurts my feelings

Mad: someone takes my stuff, someone breaks my toys

Scared: thunderstorms, horror movies, ghost stories

Younger children, can have difficulty discussing a topic as abstract as feelings. For them, feeling cards can be used. Each card has cartoon face with a feeling on it. The interviewer pulls out a card and asks:

(I): Can you make this face with your face?...Good, do you have a name for that type of face?"

If the child says "yes," the interviewer should ask the child to name the feeling, and proceed accordingly. However, if the child cannot name the feeling, the interviewer should respond:

(I): "I call this feeling happy. What makes you put on this face? What makes you happy?"

Once dialogue related to feelings has been exhausted and there has been no disclosure, the conversation should address types of touch (Bridgework Theatre, 1980; Hindman, 1983; and Beland, 1986).

(I): "Another thing I speak to children about is touching. What are some different types of touch?" or, "What do you know about touching?"

If the child provides a type of touch, the interviewer should discuss it. However if the child does not provide an answer, the interviewer should guide the dialogue through the four types of touches – good, bad, confusing, and secret. If the child discloses abuse at any stage, the interviewer should focus on gathering the details rather than completing the touch progression. The interviewer should simply introduce the first stage.

(I): "I talk about four types of touch with kids. The first type of touch is a good touch. What do you think a good touch would be?"

(I): (If child supplies an answer) "Who gives you _____?...Who else gives you good touches?...What's another type of a good touch?"

(I): (If the child does not provide an answer) "It can sometimes be hard to come up with things, so, let me help. A good touch is one that I like to get, it makes me feel good and happy. One type of touch I like is when I see my friend and we give each other high fives or shake hands. What are touches that you like to get?"

In this dialogue, the child is asked to provide an example first, but, if the child cannot, the interviewer should provide an answer and then try to encourage the child to provide his/her own. Asking the child to provide two to three answers for the type of touch and the giver of the touch in each category is beneficial. Initially, asking a child, "Who gives you..." directly seems leading. However, practice shows otherwise. Routinely, children respond, "No one," or "Nobody else," when asked for additional information.Furthermore, asking for a few examples sets a precedent for each level of this dialogue and information gathering.

Following the good touch discussion is the bad touch dialogue. Introducing it is similar to the good touch discussion.

(I): "The next type of touch I talk about is a bad touch.

What do you think a bad touch is?"

If the child is unable to define or give an example of a bad touch, the interviewer should describe a bad touch as "a touch which I do not like. It makes me feel sad or sometimes mad." A standard example of a bad touch is "when someone on the playground hits me."

The next type of touch to be examined is the confusing touch. The confusing touch is introduced to create a bridge between bad touch and secret touch. Also, it provides the interviewer one more type of touch before introducing a touch that directly implies sexual matter. The concept of the bridge is based on the simplicity of good versus bad touch. For many children, sexual abuse has good and bad components. Children often receive attention and gifts while they endure the abuse. Furthermore, children can derive physical pleasure from the sexual acts. Thus, forcing a child to see the abuse as either good or bad may not fit his/her view.

Furthermore, proposing a third type of touch before a touch that initiates the idea of sexual activity is an additional protection against leading the child.

A confusing touch is introduced the same way the good and bad touches were.

(I): "The next type of touch is called a confusing touch....It's kind of confusing to describe, too! It's one that sometimes makes me feel good and sometimes bad....It just doesn't quite fit. Who gives you confusing touches?"

The explanation of this touch can be expanded upon by facial gestures and an indi-cation of the body's role in this type of touch.

(I): "A confusing touch sometimes feels good, but it doesn't seem right in my mind, heart, and/or tummy."

An example for a confusing touch could be "when my aunt gives me a hug and won't let go!"

Because confusing touch is an abstract concept, it is not dwelled upon. Once the first three types of touches are addressed, secret touch is introduced. It is presented in the same manner as the other types. If the child is unable to provide a definition or example, the inter-viewer should proceed as follows:

(I): "The last type of touch that I talk about is a secret touch. What is a secret touch?"

(I): (If a younger child is unable to supply an example) "A secret touch is when some-one touches somebody's privates..." (The interviewer should pause to see whether the child offers any information.) "Do you know what privates are?" (Pause for answer.) "Let me get down some pictures that can help us. These show a child who doesn't have any clothes on. Kind of like when you get into a bathtub, you wouldn't wear clothes in a bathtub. That would be silly!"

(I): (If an older child is unable to supply an example) "A secret touch is when some-one touches somebody's private parts. People have lots of different names for pri-vate parts. What are your names for them?"

(I): (If the child provides his/her own words) "You know what? People use lots of dif-ferent words, and I want to make sure I clearly understand what you are calling what! I have charts that can help."

(I): (If the child does not provide an answer.) "It can be tough to just come up with things out of the blue. Sometimes having a chart can help."

The child should clearly show what privates are. However, a child should not have to do so in an exploitive fashion, by using his/her own body. Once the body drawings are intro-duced, they should be utilized as an anatomical model. (American Professional Society of the Abuse of Children, 1995). They are used to assess the child's labeling and understand-ing of body parts and the child's possible advanced knowledge of sexual acts. The inter-viewer should ask such questions as, "What do you call this part?" "What is it used for?" and, "What else does it do?" If the child resists naming the part, the interviewer should interject the anatomical name.

Starting from the picture's head, the child should be asked to provide his/her name for the body part and its function. Acknowledging three body parts before addressing the "private parts" diffuses the emphasis on genitalia.

If the child provides a pet name, a nonanatomical word for a body part, the interviewer should continue throughout the interview to call the part by the child's label. It is recommended that the interviewer write down the child's word next to the corresponding place on the chart.

Once body parts are labeled, the interviewer should explore the possibility of abuse. A variety of questions can help:

"What do you know about secret touches?"

"Who gives you secret touches?'

"Who has you give them secret touches?"

"Has anything ever happened to your [child's label for private part]?"

"Who has one of those?" (referring to opposite gender's genetalia.) If the child has not disclosed victimization by another, the drawing of the same age as the child, opposite gender should be provided.

Another option for dialogue regarding secret touch is to differentiate between good and bad secrets (Hindman, 1983).

(I): "There are good secrets, tell me one?"

(I): (child is unable to supply an example.) "A good secret would be a surprise birthday party. What would be another one?"

(I): "There are bad secrets; what would one be?"

(I): (Child does not provide example.) "A bad secret is when a child doesn't tell that he/she broke a window. What would be another one?"

Another option an interviewer has – whether used after exhausting touch dialogue without a disclosure, or used before the touch dialogue, to provide one more step before dialogue which introduces the concept of touch – is people talk. An interviewer can discuss people and events in the child's life. In alleged incest cases, the interviewer would ask the child to name those who live in his/her home. In alleged extrafamilial cases, the child should be asked to name people he/she likes and whom he/she dislikes. The child should be asked to explain his/her feelings about those people.

(I): "What does _____ do that you like?"

"What do you do with _____ that you like?"

"What does _____ do that you don't like?"

"What do you do with _____ that you don't like?"

The interviewer can then discuss activities and scenarios in which the alleged abuse may have occurred, such as the child's house, the friend's house, a park.

(I): "Who do you play with?"

(C): "Mary and Sally."

(I): "Where do you play with Mary?...Where do you play with Sally?"

(C): "At her house."

(I): "What do you play?"

(C): "We play dolls."

(I): "What else do you do at Mary's house?" or, "What else happens at Mary's house?" or, "Where do you play?"

(C): "At the park."

(I): "Boy, its been a long time since I have been to a park. What all happens at the park?...What are good things about being at the park?...What are not so good/bad things about being at the park?"

This nonleading dialogue accompanied with the previous discussions of feelings and types of touching can facilitate disclosure. It offers a nonleading presentation of events and people.

Another strategy for younger children is to talk with them about rules (Hewitt, 1995). Discuss with the child what the rules are at school and at home. Then ask him/her to name people who break rules. Once the child provides a name, he/she is encouraged to describe how the individual breaks the rules.

If a disclosure has not occurred, the multidisciplinary team needs to decide whether to terminate the interview, proceed more directly or schedule an extended forensic assessment. A team that reasonably believes the alleged abuse did not occur should use the first option. However, the other two alternatives leave open the possibility that the alleged abuse occurred. Thus, the decision should be made based on balancing the child's need for protection with the prosecution's requirements.

Experience has shown that this decision should occur without the interviewer leaving the room. Leaving the child alone can convey disinterest or rejection. Furthermore, it can make a child feel apprehensive, especially following the preceding dialogue. If team members feel that the child is at risk of further victimization, they should prompt the interviewer to proceed more directly. Highly directed questions include:

"Somebody called your caseworker because they were concerned about you. What do you think they were concerned about?"

"Somebody said you were crying a lot. How come?"

"Somebody thought you might have been hurt or touched."

"I heard that somebody gave you a secret touch."

"I heard something happened at your baby-sitter's house."

"I heard you told your daddy that someone had touched you."

"I heard you went to the doctor. What for?"

If this line of questioning does not generate a disclosure, the decision to conduct an extended forensic assessment or to dismiss the child should be made. Regardless what route is chosen, the child's need for protection should be determined. Whether or not a disclosure has occurred or an extended forensic assessment has been selected, the information-gathering portion of the interview has ceased.

REFERENCES:

American Professional Society on the Abuse of Children. (1995). *Practice guidelines: Use of anatomical dolls on child sexual abuse assessments.* Chicago: American Professional Society on the Abuse of Children.

Beland, K. (1986). *Talk about touching: Personal safety for preschoolers and kindergartners.* Washington, DC: Committee for Children.

Bridgework Theater. (1980). Big bear, little bear child abuse prevention play. Goshen, IN: Bridgework Theater.

Faller, K. (1990). Types of questions for assessing allegation of sexual abuse. *The APSAC Advisor, 3,* 5-7.

Hewitt, S. (1995). *Small voices... Big wound: Assessing and managing cases of sexually abused young children.* Seminar coordinated by The Creche Child and Family Centre and the Catholic Children's Aid Society of Metropolitan Toronto. Toronto, Canada.

Hindman, J. (1983). *A very touching book.* Ontario, OR: Alexandria Associates.

Chapter 12

CHILD PROTECTION, CHILD ABUSE PREVENTION, AND CLOSURE

As previously discussed, all three phases of the interview have importance. Often, the closing phase can be hurried, which is not advantageous to the child's recovery, the child's protection, nor the possible prosecution of the case. A child needs to feel as though he/she, as an individual, is of value, not just his/her relaying of the details. Taking the time to formally close the interview can convey that message.

An initial question for introducing this phase of the interview is, "What have I forgotten to ask you?" Frequently children will indicate that all the pertinent questions have been raised. However, on a significant number of occasions, a child will supply further details. As such, this question is worth utilizing. Furthermore, this question can be used as a cue to the other multidisciplinary team members that the interviewer is about to close the interview, and that they should review their notes and relay any further questions or points that need clarification.

Two other simple, yet good, questions are, "Is there anything that you're not supposed to tell me?" and, "Did anyone tell you what to say or not to say in here today?" The first question can be asked either in the rapport-building phase or at closure. An interviewer must weigh when to ask it. If asked too soon, a child can become intimidated. However, it can also catch a young child off guard, thus eliciting information. If asked during the closure phase, after the child has disclosed, it provides an avenue for "extremely taboo" details to be introduced.

The latter question provides an opportunity for a child to relay information from either a supportive parent who may have said, "You tell the truth in there," or a coercive parent, who may have facilitated a fictitious report.

Whether or not the child has disclosed abuse, he/she should be praised for his/her cooperation and work, not for what he/she said. Use phrases as:

"Thank you for putting up with all my questions."

"You did a nice job in staying in here, I know it can be hard to talk with someone you don't know that well."

"Thanks for coming here today, and for taking the time and energy to talk with me."

In all of the above phrases, the child's actions are being praised, not the content of what he/she has said. This is crucial, for the child's interview is just one part of the investigation and further investigation needs to occur. Also, if the child wished to disclose more later, he/she would not be restricted from doing so. And finally, none of these comments indicates the believability or lack thereof of the child's statements.

A second ingredient in closure is mutual sharing. An interviewer should not disclose personal information about him/herself, but rather share with the child the potential course of the investigation. However, an interviewer should avoid speculating or making false promises. A child has entrusted his/her life to the interviewer and deserves to be able to regain some control by learning what may occur. An interviewer should supply only general steps, because he/she has no power over what will happen. Simply state:

"I can't guarantee what all will happen, but I do know that the detective and caseworker will go and talk with your parent. And then they will talk with (alleged perpetrator's name). How do you feel about that?...What concerns you the most about what will happen?"

The above question/statement does not tell the child specifically what will happen. This is crucial, because especially in a time of crisis, a child is likely to hold onto every word said by the interviewer. Thus, if the interviewer misleads the child, he/she could feel betrayed. If a child is to return for an extended forensic assessment (see Chapter 13), the child should be informed of it at this time.

Another vital goal of the closing portion of the interview is an attempt to assess the nonoffending parent's ability to support and protect the child. The child's perception of the parent's and family's response can generate poignant and useful information. Uncomplicated questions such as

"How do you think things will be now that you told someone?...How do you think your mom will respond?..Your dad?..Your brothers and sisters?" or

"What things/people/situations do you think will cause you problems?...Whom can you turn to for help?"

These question can help to ascertain what level of protection the child needs. For if a child discloses and are returned to a nonsupportive or accusatory environment, recantation and further abuse are highly probable. Not only can valuable information be obtained by asking these questions, the child can feel supported and discuss fears and work out solutions. This does not mean that the interviewer should do therapy; these roles should remain separate. Rather, the interviewer can prepare the child to leave the interview room equipped to face his/her reality.

Empowerment should be a focus of the entire interview process. Although potentially horrifying, a child's disclosure facilitates his/her progression from "victim" to "survivor." The child's voice, which has been muffled, is finally audible. During the closure phase, a few steps can contribute to the child's ongoing empowerment.

One basic way to relinquish the power of the interviewer and confer it on the child is to ask whether he/she has any concerns to raise.

"You know, I've been asking all the questions, you should have your turn for asking. What would you like to know?"

Without fail, children will ask about the interviewer's sexual habits or likelihood of childhood victimization. As previously stated, a child's question often does not mean he/she wants to know the answer. So, an appropriate response would be:

"Good question. I'm curious how come you would like to know that information?"

If a child says, "Because," a suitable response for an interviewer is:

"I am aware you are curious, but talking about mutually agreed upon sexual acts between two consenting and old enough people is something they discuss only between themselves. It is different than talking with someone about an abusive or unfair sexual act."

"I know it seems weird that you've been asked to talk about your past, and now I won't talk about whether I was abused. But abuse is a topic one discusses with professionals, either an interviewer like me or a therapist. Talking with friends can be tricky. Unfortunately, sometimes people let things out and it can really hurt. Does that make sense?"..."What's really important is if abuse is happening, it gets reported to the right people so it can stop, because no one deserves to get abused."

Another significant aspect that needs to be discussed with older children is the potential effects of the abuse and the system's involvement. Plainly asking the child, "How do you think [the abuse] has affected you?" can let the interviewer know what concerns the child. Also, a review of the behavioral inventory provided by the parent (see Chapter 14) can provide the interviewer with some idea of what the presenting consequences of the alleged abuse are. The child should have a chance to discuss with the interviewer an appropriate description of what is occurring and what will make them feel bad. Just knowing potential consequences ahead of time can decrease the anxiety a child may encounter (Perry, 1995) and decreases the chance the child will be caught off guard.

Another area of empowerment occurs in tidying the interview room. It is advantageous to have the child help clean the room. Symbolically, if the child has disclosed, this allows him/her to put everything in order. He/she is not leaving items that were used in his/her disclosure out in the open. If dolls or charts were used, they are put away properly. This means that the charts are placed in a folder and the cover closed. The dolls should be reclothed and returned to their bag. Nothing should be left in a vulnerable state.

Whether or not the child has disclosed abuse, a brief dialogue on prevention is valuable. Because various types of touch have been introduced, closure on the topic is needed. If a child has not been abused, the touch topic can be confusing if it is left unresolved. Furthermore, it is a responsible gesture to address protection with this captive audience. For a child who may have been abused but is not disclosing, this dialogue can convey that when they are ready to disclose, someone will listen; and for a child who has disclosed, it informs them that if there is more to tell or if they are revictimized, they will know what to do. The dialogue includes the following questions and comments from the interviewer:

"You know how we were talking about bad, secret, and confusing touches today. Who could you go to if you got one of those?"

(If child relays names) "What would you say to them?"

(If child does not supply names) "It can be tough to think about. How about your teacher? Who else do you trust?"

Just a few minutes on this topic can yield significant benefits.

Finally, a child should determine, within reason, when he/she is ready to return to the waiting area. Does the child need a few minutes to regroup before facing his/her family members? Or is the child just plain ready to get out of the interviewing room? An uncomplicated question such as, "Do you want to go back to the waiting room/to mom or would you like to stay in here for a few minutes?" can help.

If the child decides to remain in the room, the interviewer needs to set a limit of three to five minutes, let the child know the time frame, and keep the child aware of the time remaining.

The closure phase of an interview is usually brief. However, these minutes can make a significant difference not only to the child's recovery process, but also to his/her response to the intervening system, which may need his/her involvement later.

REFERENCES:

Perry, B. (1995). Childhood Trauma Treatment Program seminar: *Psychological and medical responses to childhood trauma.* Bolingbrook, IL.

Chapter 13

EXTENDED FORENSIC ASSESSMENT

Initial investigative interviews can result in a disclosure. It is ludicrous to expect every abused child to disclose the first time he/she is interviewed. The lack of a disclosure may stem from denial, fear, shock, or that no abuse occurred. A child may need more time to develop trust in the interviewer. As has been discussed, disclosure of details is a process. Unfortunately, naive interviewers and team members will dismiss a case if the child does not immediately disclose, rather than, if the situation warrants, conducting an extended forensic assessment (EFA).

Whether to conduct an EFA is a team decision. An EFA is warranted in cases in which 1) a child has made a partial disclosure and clarification is necessary; and 2) a child has not made a disclosure but significant indicators – behavioral, familial, or collateral – highly suggest sexual abuse.

An EFA allows an abused child time after the initial shock and denial to regroup and possibly relay information he/she simply was not able to talk about at the first meeting.

The EFA is a valuable component of both the investigation and treatment of child sexual abuse. The EFA addresses whether the alleged abuse occurred, and if so, the extent and nature of the abuse. It focuses on the child and family's level of functioning and needs. Although an investigative interview attends to these as well, the EFA allows the child to disclose this information during duration-limited multiple sessions. Furthermore, the EFA more thoroughly identifies the effects of the victimization or other dysfunction/trauma in the child's life and recommends a child abuse or problem-specific treatment plan.

A child should have mastered certain developmental tasks before an EFA is conducted. The child's speech should be moderately intelligible and he/she should have sufficient language skills. The child should know or be able to learn such concepts as who, what, and types of touches. The child should also know or be able to learn names for the body parts.

Ideally, the child should be able to play representationally with materials. However this should not be rigidly adhered to, for it is believed that children under the age of 4 cannot. (Hewitt, 1995).

The EFA can provide a continuum of care for the child and family. Instead of curtailing an investigation when a disclosure is not produced, the EFA allows for the investigation and intervention to continue.

There has been debate over who should conduct the EFA (Gil & Amacher, 1992). One view is that a therapist should both assess and treat. The thought is that the establishment of the therapeutic relationship and the therapist's unconditional acceptance will encourage communication. The other perspective is to have the interviewer conduct the assessment and a therapist provide the therapy afterward. The rationale for this view is that the processes are distinct. The goal of an assessment is to determine the likelihood of abuse. Thus, the interviewer must confront and challenge the child's statements and be more task-oriented, unlike the therapist and the therapy process. Because the EFA is forensic in nature, it is recommended that the same interviewer conduct the initial interview and the EFA.

The goal of the EFA is to discover the truth gradually. The process of disclosure is accentuated. This does not decrease the importance of the forensic elements. An EFA is conducted in the same forensically sound manner as the initial investigative interview. However, beyond the longer period for rapport building and engagement, it also allows the interviewer to employ more tools and activities with the child.

Tools and activities utilized during the EFA should be based on the child's developmental abilities. There is no particular order in which the tools should be used, except that as like in the interviewing process, the focus should move from broad toward specific. Tools considered suitable for an EFA include:

markers, crayons, and paper

worksheets and flashcards

rag dolls

anatomically detailed dolls and charts

board games (therapeutic and nontherapeutic)

dollhouse and figurines

puppets

Markers, crayons, and paper can be used for free drawing or structured activities, such as a touch continuum (Hewitt, 1995), the seven-stage drawing (adapted from Robinson, 1986), feelings inside and outside, and the lifeline exercise.

Touch continuum: The interviewer will need three pieces of paper and markers. The interviewer asks the child to guide him/her in drawing faces that represent happy, sad, mad, scared. The four faces are drawn on a single sheet of paper. On the second sheet, the interviewer draws the grid shown in Figure 1, and on the third sheet the interviewer draws the questions shown in Figure 2.

Figure 1

HUG	TICKLE	SPANK
KISS/TASTE	HIT	WHERE DO YOU GO POTTY (FRONT AND BACK)

Figure 2

WHO DO YOU TOUCH? WHO HAS YOU TOUCH THEM?

The interviewer should try hard to make the figurine representational of the child, i.e., same color and length of hair. The interviewer should guide the child through the Figure 1 frames.

(I): "Who _____s you?"

"Where?"

"How do you feel?"

Once completed, the interviewer and child should progress to Figure 2.

(I): "Whom do you touch?"

"Who has you touch them?"

If the child does not respond or responds negatively, the interviewer should proceed.

(I): "Do you give your dad hugs?"

"Do you hold your mom's hand?"

"Who else?"

If a disclosure is initiated with this or any other activity, detail gathering should begin.

Seven-stage drawings: This activity is lengthy. If an interviewer determines it cannot be completed in one session, the number of drawings should be reduced. Start with benign topics, escalate to a potentially volatile subject, and deintensify with safer themes. This process should be executed in one session. In the seven-stage activity, the child is instructed to draw:

1. Your favorite day/weather.

2. A tree.

3. A house.

4. Your family doing something (alleged incest), or your friends/neighborhood/class/ a bunch of people/etc. doing something together.

5. You and the alleged perpetrator doing something.

6. You doing something that makes you happy.

7. Anything you would like to draw.

The pictures are used as a catalyst for conversation, not as a diagnostic or interpretive tool. They can be discussed after each is drawn, or cumulatively at the end. This choice is based on the child's attention span and the impact of the activity.

Feelings inside and out: This activity uses one piece of paper folded in half, making each half 8.5 inches by 5.5 inches. The child is asked to draw a picture of himself/herself on the front.

(I): "Draw a picture of yourself without the face drawn in."

(Once the picture is complete) "Now draw your face, how everyone sees you. How you show yourself to everyone."

When finished, the child is asked to open the paper and draw another self-portrait.

(I): "This time draw yourself, but it's the self no one else sees, the feelings you have inside that people don't see. This is kind of like an X-ray machine."

Once both are complete, they are discussed.

Lifeline exercise: The interviewer should tape several pieces of paper together to create a long roll, on which a horizontal line is drawn. the child or the interviewer should start at the left side of the page and mark intervals from birth to the present age. Then, the child is asked to write or draw in significant events. Once the lifeline is complete, the interviewer asks the child to write or place the appropriate feeling face by each event and by each age range. Then either at the end or at each milestone, the incident and the accompanying feelings are discussed.

Crayons and markers can also be used with premade worksheets. Worksheets create a respite from direct dialogue between the child and interviewer and are familiar to the child because they are used in school. Frequently, it is easier for the child to initially write or draw on paper, and then discuss it. As such, several worksheets have been incorporated into the EFA.

Three workbooks (Spinal-Robinson & Wickham-Easton, 1992A, 1992B, 1992C), although designed for use in treatment, have several worksheets that are applicable to a forensic assessment. The workbooks, "Flip Flops," "Cart Wheels," and "High Tops: Workbooks for Children Who Have Been Sexually Abused," are divided into age-appropriate activities. Some of the same activities are found in each book, but they are altered for the various ages. The following exercises are appropriate:

Wishes: A child colors in a lantern similar to Aladdin's and is asked to fill in three wishes, which are then discussed.

Meet my family: This worksheet allows the child to answer questions about the positive and negative aspects of his/her household. It is a good icebreaker for cases involving alleged incest or abuse by someone in the home.

Getting to know yourself/How I see myself/ Promoting yourself: Again, this is a good icebreaker. This worksheet asks questions comparable to those asked during the rapport-building phase. This worksheet helps set the stage for more direct worksheets.

Finding feelings word find/Measuring feelings/Feeling sentences completion/Knowing what you feel: These activity sheets provide an alternate way to discuss feelings. They reduce the monotony of repeated feeling questions.

How to protect yourself: This and other worksheets can be used in post-disclosure discussions or as a tool in discussing prevention.

Interviewers should review other activity books for exercises.

Other worksheets adapted from the works of James (1989) and flashcards adapted from the writings of Cavanaugh Johnson (1995), Cunningham and MacFarlane (1991), and Spinal-Robinson and Wickham-Easton (1992A, 1992B, & 1992C) have been adapted for the EFA.

In the first three exercises, the interviewer helps the child supply answers for the lines and explores the child's responses. In the touch thermometer activity, the interviewer guides the child as he/she enter and discuss a range of touches. Initial dialogue addresses "cool/all right" touches, which are placed at the bottom of the thermometer, followed by "middle/in between" touches, which are entered and described. Lastly, "heated/tense" touches are explored and written in near the top of the thermometer.

Beyond worksheets, flashcards can be a valuable resource. Cards can facilitate dialogue about feelings and types of secrets.Using pictures from old library books and magazines, or from premade feeling face charts, can stimulate discussion. These can be used in various activities. Faces can be cut out and taped to brightly colored cardboard shapes and placed in a bag. The interviewer and the child can take turns drawing a face and discussing a time in which they felt that way. A spin wheel with face pictures placed in each section can be created to generate another playful approach. Finally, picture cards that portray various interactions can be utilized.

(I): "How do you think the people are feeling in this picture?"

"When have you ever felt that way/that feeling?"

The final type of flashcards incorporated into the EFA is related to secrets. The cards are made with pictures that depict scenes in which a secret can be seen and providing the child with an accompanying narrative. The secrets should include:

a birthday gift

a surprise birthday party

someone doing an anonymous kind gesture

someone cheating on a test

someone stealing

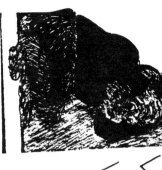

WHAT PEOPLE'S BODIES DO
WHEN THEY ARE SCARED . . . .

REACTION   YES   NO   HOW OLD   EVENT

--- --- ---

SHAKING

WET PANTS

CRIED

GOT REAL QUIET

SCREAMED

WHAT ELSE?

BAD, MEAN, ROTTEN THINGS THAT CAN HAPPEN TO KIDS...

_____

_____

_____

_____

_____

_____

_____

_____

The Touch Thermometer

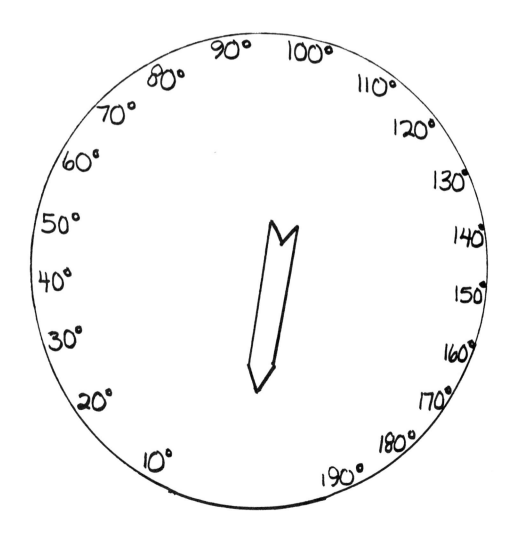

Once these cards are shown, a logical sequence is for the interviewer to have a few blank cards and to initiate the child's relaying of other types of secrets.

(I): "Those were a few types of secrets. What are other types?...What are secrets you are asked to keep?"

The dolls, rag and anatomically detailed, and the charts are used in the same manner as in the initial interview. They should be introduced only as a demonstration or clarification tool.

Board games can be used for either information gathering or as a respite from the intensity of dialogue and structured activities.

Edited use of therapeutic board games such as "Let's Talk About Touching" (Cavanaugh Johnson, 1992A), "Let's Talk About Touching in the Family" (Cavanaugh Johnson, 1992B), "Pick and Tell Game" (Gardner, 1994) and "The Talking, Feeling, Doing Game" (Gardner, 1973) can render a beneficial exchange of information. An edited use implies that the non-leading cards from these games are used and the strict rules of the games are not followed fastidiously. More direct question cards may be introduced at a later session if the team determines the necessity.

Three other non-manufactured games created for the EFA process are the telling game, the sentence completion game, and the people game.

The telling game is a poster board with two tracks drawn on it. Each track has twenty spaces. Any board game that has a track can be used. The child and the interviewer each have a playing piece, which is moved along the board. Each takes a turn drawing a question card from the pile. There are twenty-four scenarios.

1. A baby sitter talks on the telephone with her boyfriend and tells the child not to tell.

2. A baby sitter will let a child stay up late if he/she takes off all his/her clothes.

3. A child's brother/sister hits him/her real hard.

4. A child's brother/sister/friend tells him/her about a surprise gift he/she bought.

5. A mom eats a whole bag of cookies and asks the child not to tell the dad.

6. A boy steals two candy bars from the store and tells his friend that he will share them if the friend doesn't tell his mom.

7. An adult touches a child's private parts and says he/she will hurt the child if he/she tells.

8. An adult touches a child's private parts and tells the child not to tell anyone.

9. A girl/boy breaks her/his mom's glass bowl.

10. A dad always comes into the bathroom when the child is naked.

11. A sister always comes into the brother's room without knocking.

12. A child sees three hot-air balloons in the sky.

13. A little girl/boy is being touched on her/his private parts.

14. A child is made to touch an adult's private parts.

15. A child went to the zoo with a friend.

16. A dog ate a lady's shoe.

17. A dog ran through the neighbor's flower garden.

18. A child hits a baseball that breaks the neighbor's window.

19. A grandmother gives a child cookies and ice cream before dinner.

20. A sister tells her brother that she is going to run away from home.

21. A child's brother/sister has a big party at the home while the parents are out of town.

22. A girl/boy is smoking cigarettes in her/his bedroom.

23. A boy gives his vegetables to the dog when his mom isn't looking.

24. A baby sitter goes out with her friends and leaves the child at home alone.

The child either reads or is read the scenario, and then is asked:

"Should you tell?"

"Who?"

"What do you think will happen?"

"Has anything like this ever happened to you?"

The last question is asked at the discretion of the interviewer. Potentially leading questions can be removed from the deck before the game begins. After answering, the player draws a number card that indicates how many spaces to move. The number cards range from one to three. The game ends when the first player reaches the finish line.

A similar game is sentence completion. It is played the same way, except the cards drawn are sentences that need to be completed.

1. People don't like me when...

2. People do like me when...

3. Being a boy is nice because...

4. I feel hurt when...

5. Sometimes I think I'm...

6. I think I am capable at...

7. If someone gave me a nice surprise, it'd be...

8. Something I need to improve on is...

9. Something that is important to me is...

10. What I dislike the most about school is...

11. When I lose an argument or game, I feel...

12. Something I have in common with others who are my age is...

13. Being a girl is nice because...

14. If I could be someone else, I'd be...

15. Something that frightens me is...

16. The thing about me I'd like to change is...

17. Something I'd like to try is...

18. Something I believe strongly is...because...

19. I really am...

20. The best thing about me is...

21. The worst thing about my family is...

22. I'm good at...

23. A sad thing that happened to me is...

24. Something that I like about myself is...

25. When I'm with my friends I like to...

26. When I am alone, I...

27. The best thing about my family is...

28. Something that made me mad is...

29. The person who makes me mad is...

30. One of my talents is...

31. If I could change anything about my family it would be...

32. If I could change anything in my life it would be...

33. An important decision I have made is...

34. I wish I...

35. I feel happy when...

36. I am scared about...

37. Something that concerns me is...

38. The one thing that I would like to stop is...

39. The best thing that ever happened to me is...

40. One thing that bothers me is...

In contrast to the previous game, the questions are so open-ended that cards do not need to be omitted.

The third game is the people game. It is played the same as the two other games. However, the cards address people in the child's life.

Who are people I like?

Who are people I don't like?

Who are safe people?

Who are unsafe people?

Who hurts me?

Who makes me feel good?

Who makes me feel bad?

Who makes me feel scared?

Whom am I afraid of?

Whom do I like to be with?

Who is my friend?

Who sometimes hurts me?

Who makes me feel better?

General board games can also be incorporated into the EFA process as a recess from the focused dialogue and activities. Those that a child might play with family and friends can be introduced periodically during the EFA.

The final category of tools includes the dollhouse and figurines and puppets. These tools are vehicles for communication, not objects for fantasy play. They should be stored and introduced only when they will be used. The dollhouse is best used as a demonstration for Gil's Typical Day exercise (National Training Program on Effective Treatment Approaches, 1992).

This exercise is an effective way to elicit information about the child's life and family. The child selects a figurine to represent each person who lives at his/her home, including him/herself. The interviewer then directs the child through a day.

(I): "Okay, it's early morning, just before everyone wakes up. Where is everybody?"

The interviewer then inquires about the figurines' activities and interactions. Meals, baths, responsibilities, after-school games/activities, bedtime rituals, and post bedtime activities are helpful targets. Additionally, asking about people's feelings towards others can yield beneficial information. Finally, the child should be asked about appropriate and inappropriate touches.

(I): "Who gives the best hugs?"

"What kind of touches do you like to get?"

"What kind of touches do you not like to get?"

Puppets can be used as the child's voice. Some children prefer to have the animal placed in front of their faces while talking, others like to use the animal as the mediator between the interviewer and themselves. If the puppets are used, the interviewer must reiterate the necessity of only telling about the truth, and that the animal/puppet is being used to assist the dialogue.

The above activities are not the only ones that can be used in an extended forensic assessment. Rather, they are a starting point. Additional activities should be adapted as appropriate.

While the assessment is under way, an advocate or another professional should work with the nonoffending parent. This relationship is twofold. First, it offers support. Second, it provides an opportunity to gather more information regarding the child and his/her environment.

The nonoffending parent provides indispensable information through an extended questionnaire (see Appendix A); a review of the Child Behavioral Inventory, adapted from a questionnaire used by Conte (1988) (see Appendix B) or the completion of the Achenbach Child Behavioral Checklist (Achenbach & Edelbrock, 1983); and the completion of the Children's Behavior Survey,(CSBI) Version 3 (Friedrich, 1992). If a nonoffending parent documents behavioral changes in the child, the professional should inquire about a time line for those changes. The EFA parent's questionnaire is conducted in an interview format. Rather than having the parent write the answer, the professional conducts an interview at each session of the assessment. The Child Behavioral Inventory typically is completed before the initial interview, and it is reviewed during the EFA process for further clarification. This tool has not been tested for reliability and validity, but can be used as an information tool that facilitates dialogue. For a standardized tool, the Achenbach can be considered.

In choosing among these tools it must be remembered that there is no single item or cluster of items that can unequivocally determine whether a child has or has not been abused. However, a combination of the CSBI, a behavioral inventory, a comprehensive and meticulous clinical interview(s) with the child, and an exhaustive review with the nonoffending parent and collateral sources can help the interviewer arrive at the truth and validate the interviewer's findings.

Upon completion of the extended forensic assessment, an extensive report should be compiled by the interviewer (see Appendix C). The report should discuss the findings in extensive detail and provide thorough intervention recommendations. This report should be disseminated to the members of the multidisciplinary team. The nonoffending parent should have an opportunity to meet with either the advocate or the interviewer to review the report and the recommendations before or as it is circulated to the professionals involved in the investigation.

REFERENCES:

Achenbach, T., & Edelbrock, C. (1983). *Manual for the child behavior checklist and revised child behavior profile.* VT: University of Vermont Department of Psychiatry.

Cavanaugh-Johnson, T. (1992A). *Let's talk about touching: A therapeutic game* (2nd ed.). Pasadena, CA: Author.

Cavanaugh-Johnson, T.(1992B). *Let's talk about touching in the family: A therapeutic game.* Pasadena, CA: Author.

Cavanaugh-Johnson, T. (1995). *Treatment exercises for child abuse victims and children with sexual behavior problems.* Pasadena, CA: Author.

Conte, J. (1988). Questionnaire used for professional survey on evaluating children's reports of sexual abuse.

Cunningham, C., & MacFarlane, K. (1991). *When children molest children: Group treatment strategies for young sexual abusers.* Orwell, VT: Safer Society Press.

Friedrich, W. (1992). *Children's behavior survey,* Version 3. MN: Mayo Medical School.

Gardner, R. (1973). *The talking, feeling, doing game.* Cresskill, NJ: Creative Therapeutics.

Gardner, R. (1994). *The pick and tell game.* Cresskill, NJ: Creative Therapeutics.

James, B. (1989). *Treating traumatized children: New insights and creative interventions.* Lexington, MA: Lexington Books.

Gil, E., & Amacher, E. (1992). *National training program on effective treatment approaches.* Huntsville, AL: National Children's Advocacy Center.

Hewitt, S. (1995). *Small voices... Big wound: Assessing and managing cases of sexually abused young children.* Seminar coordinated by The Creche Child and Family Centre and the Catholic Children's Aid Society of Metropolitan Toronto. Toronto, Canada.

National Training Program on Effective Treatment Approaches. (1992). Huntsville, AL: National Children's Advocacy Center.

Robinson, S., (1986). Internship supervision dialogue. Child Sexual Abuse Treatment and Training Center, Bolingbrook, IL.

Spinal-Robinson, P., & Wickham-Easton, R. (1992A). *Cartwheels: A workbook for children who have been sexually abused.* Notre Dame, IN: Jalice Publishers.

Spinal-Robinson, P., & Wickham-Easton, R. (1992B). *High tops: A workbook for children who have been sexually abused.* Notre Dame, IN: Jalice Publishers.

Spinal-Robinson, P., & Wickham-Easton, R. (1992C). *Flip flops: A workbook for children who have been sexually abused.* Notre Dame, IN: Jalice Publishers.

Chapter 14

RESISTANT CHILDREN

Sometimes just getting the child into the interviewing room is the interviewer's biggest obstacle. Quite often a child is hesitant to enter the interviewing room, and understandably so. Most children have never been in an interviewing room, and they may be unsure and have frightening expectations of what occurs there. Other children indeed may have heard of an interviewing room and are fully aware of the burden that will be placed upon them when they enter the room.

Strategies that assist in reducing children's concerns and help them enter the room include:

1. If the child is old enough, process his/her concerns. Validate his/her hesitance, and honestly discuss his/her feelings. For many children who have been abused, few people in their lives have taken the time to ask them how they are feeling. If the interviewer takes a few minutes to address the child as a human being rather than an object, great steps can be made not only in the interview, but more importantly in the child's recovery.

2. If a child is playing with toys in the waiting area and does not want to leave, discourage the child from bringing the toy with him/her into the interviewing room. Allow this only as a last resort. Toys that have not been identified as interviewing aids can be used by a child for distraction. These distractive toys can create a power struggle between the interviewer and the child.

Explain to the child that the toys will be in the waiting room upon his/her return. If this explanation is not sufficient, agree with the child to hide the toy where it will be safe until the two of you finish the interview.

3. Play on the child's curiosity. Ask, "Have you ever seen an interviewing room?" or, "Have you ever seen a kid's talking room?" This way, the interviewer turns the transition into a mini-adventure.

However, typically a few children will answer "yes." If this happens, the interviewer should validate the child's answer, and ask the child to describe his/her room. Then, the interviewer should explain, "Oh, yours sounds pretty neat. Mine's a little different. Do you know how mine is different? Let's go see." The interviewer should avoid posing questions that could lead a child to answering "no." If that happens, the interviewer is stuck or forced to invalidate what the child has said. For example, if the interviewer in this situation says, "Would you like to go see how my room is different?" and the child says "no," what can the interviewer do?

4. If a child appears to be relying on his/her parent's support and endorsement, ask the parent, "Is it all right for _____ to come with me to my interviewing room?" A word of caution, however: Before using this strategy, ascertain that the parent will be supportive and not strongly authoritative.

If the first step is unsuccessful, ask the parent if he/she will escort you and the child to the room's doorway. If the parent accepts, turn to the child and say, "Your [mom/dad] will join us as we walk back. Let's go."

If the parent must enter the room, have him/her leave once the child has become acclimated. It compromises the discovery of truth and the disclosure process to have the parent present. The rationale for this belief is multifaceted: First, the child may be worried about disappointing the parent by disclosing the activities in which he or she participated. Second, the child may feel exploited by several individuals watching his or her disclosure. Third, even a supportive parent may share the specific details of the disclosure with the alleged perpetrator. Fourth, the interviewer cannot control the parent's reactions to disclosure, thus the interviewer's attention could be shifted from the child to the parent. Fifth, a parent's reaction to the disclosure may have an impact on the child. Sixth, the parent may be involved directly or indirectly in the alleged abuse.

If the parent must remain, ask him/her to sit behind and off to the side of the child, thus prohibiting eye contact and touch. Once the child is in the room, it is important to engage him/her in a nonthreatening activity, such as drawing. Having a one-on-one dialogue with a stranger can be quite intimidating to a child, and may lead him/her to withdraw from the conversation or leave the room.

Once the child has adjusted, the interviewer should arrange to have the parent leave the room quietly. The parent's departure should not be brought to the child's attention by saying, for example,

"Is it okay for your mom to leave now?" or, "How nice it is that you are in here without your father."

If a child is adamant that he/she will not go into the interviewing room, do not force him/her. Forcing a child breeds further resistance and greatly decreases the likelihood of dialogue. Not only is it detrimental to the interview, it may also be traumatic for the child. Rather, the interviewer should see whether he/she can get the child to look at the room from the doorway, and then make arrangements for the interview to occur the next day or hours later. Some children need extra time to develop trust in the interviewer and the situation. It is a mistake for an interviewer to assume that a child automatically trusts him/her and that the child knows that the interviewer is there to help him/her. It is usually just the opposite.

Using a "two times up, you're out" rule can be effective. If the interviewer has succeeded in getting the hesitant child into the room but the child frequently goes to the door, caution is needed. The interviewer should not bribe the child into remaining, by saying, for example, "You can go out after we talk," or, "We have to talk first." Rather, the interviewer should acknowledge that the child is approaching the door, and assess (especially with younger children) whether the child should be allowed to check on his/her parent and act accordingly. An encounter might go as follows:

(I): "Mary, I see you're going toward the door. How come?"

(C): (Silence)

(I): "I sure would like to get to know you. Let's draw" (pulls out paper and crayons and begins drawing).

At this point either the child engages in drawing or keeps struggling with the need to leave. If it is the latter:

(I): "Mary, why don't we go and check to see if your mom is okay, and then we'll come back."

If the child needs to leave the room twice, the interview should be rescheduled.

When a child controls the interview through distraction, such as lying down, playing with a toy or spitting, the interviewer should attempt to regain control. It helps to simply say to the child, "Joe, I am having a hard time talking. It would help if we could sit down over here together and talk for a few minutes." Or, "Mary, in this room we talk. Let's sit here." After several failed attempts, it may be worth considering another session. In either scenario, there is the likelihood that the interviewer will get into a power struggle with the child, which will yield a nonproductive, nontherapeutic interview.

Remember, one of the goals of interviewing is to minimize the potential harm to the child. A child who feels forced to be present is unlikely to divulge information, and a child who appears to have been bribed does not produce a forensically sound case.

Chapter 15

ASSESSING THE NONOFFENDING PARENT

When there are allegations that a child has been sexually assaulted or traumatized, whether incest or extrafamilial, a nonoffending parent can respond in any number of ways. Often the referral and disclosure cause a nonoffending parent to feel as though his/her world has been turned upside down.

A child's disclosure can challenge all the resources of a nonoffending parent. This makes it extremely difficult for the parent to help the child. Frequently a nonoffending parent is completely focused on coping with the immediate crisis of the disclosure and its short-term ramifications. So for the interviewer and the interdisciplinary team to better serve the child and conduct a comprehensive investigation, they need to assist and assess a nonoffending parent's feelings and gather collateral information.

A nonoffending parent may experience a wide range of emotions (Cammaert, 1988; Ovaris, 1995; Sgroi & Dana, 1982). A nonoffending parent's reaction will dramatically vary, based on the dynamics of the case and the personalities of those involved.

A parent identified as nonoffending, especially in incest but also in extrafamilial cases, can be placed on a continuum of participation. At one extreme, a nonoffending parent is oblivious to his/her child's abuse. Because of their own issues, some nonoffending parents are not emotionally available to the child and do not see or even consider there to be a problem. Less extreme is the nonoffending parent who knows something is not quite right. He/she is aware that the child is behaving differently and that family dynamics have changed. However, the possibility of abuse has not dawned on him/her.

Bordering this category is the nonoffending parent who is quite aware that things are not normal and suspects that the cause is abuse. The next category of parents, who are not clearly nonoffending, are those who know abuse has occurred and allow it to continue. Some parents in this group may be conspirators or co-perpetrators.

The final group is nonoffending parents who become aware of the abuse and do something about it, i.e., bring his/her child to the attention of the system.

Equally diverse are nonoffending parents' reactions to their child's disclosures and the investigatory and intervening system. Common reactions of nonoffending parents include:

1. **Denial.** The nonoffending parent may deny that the alleged abuse occurred. The parent may minimize, a form of denial, saying there was little harm done. "I was abused and it didn't bother me, so it shouldn't bother my child," or, "She was only touched three times; she'll get over it." Finally, the nonoffending parent may acknowledge the abuse and its harm but believe that outside help is unneccesary to recovery. "Yes, he was abused, but we don't need any assistance from the outside. We'll get over this just fine on our own."

2. **Jealousy.** This response often occurs in symbiotic abuse relationships (Groth, 1979). The abuse relationship mimics that of lovers or boyfriend/girlfriend. As a result, the nonoffending parent may come to view the child as "the other woman" and become resentful. One result of this view is that the nonoffending parent becomes enraged at the child for "seducing" the offender. Often, it is easier for the nonoffending parent to become angry at the child than at the perpetrator. Such a parent often believes that a child gives unconditional love, but a partner's love may be harder to obtain; thus, the nonoffending parent may wish to retain it.

3. **Anger.** The nonoffending parent may feel anger on several levels. He/she may be angry at him/herself for failing to protect the child and missing the signs of abuse. Sometimes, the nonoffending parent may be aggravated at the child for not having disclosed sooner. Many times, the nonoffending parent's anger may be a disguise for the embarrassment he/she may feel over his/her failure to detect the abuse.

4. **Insecurity.** The nonoffending parent may fear being left alone. The belief is, "My child will be out of the home in eight years, and then I will have no one if I don't side with the alleged perpetrator."

5. **Helplessness/lack of assertiveness.** The nonoffending parent is entering a world about which he/she usually knows little. He/she has little idea of what is expected of him/her and may be fearful of losing the child through foster placement. Characteristically, the initial investigation is focused on the child, the alleged perpetrator, and discovering the truth regarding the allegation. Frequently, the nonoffending parent feels invisible.

6. **Shock, numbness, and repulsion.** Many nonoffending parents were victimized in childhood, and often the child's disclosure propels him/her to revisit his/her own victimization and related feelings. Therefore, it is not surprising when the nonoffending parent dissociates from the current situation. It's a coping mechanism with which he/she is familiar. The nonoffending parent also may be repulsed about hearing of the acts that occurred. It is one thing to hear sexual acts described; however, when the acts victimize one's child it can be unbearable.

7. **Guilt and self-blame.** False parenting beliefs may lead the nonoffending parent to feel as though he/she has total responsibility for the child's complete well-being. Such misconceptions include: "Parents have total responsibility for everything that happens to their children. Good parents have happy, healthy children. If a parent is around, i.e., alive, no harm can come to the child. A child's well-being is proof of a parent's love" (Ovaris, 1995). These beliefs further spiral the nonoffending parent into despair and guilt.

8. **Hurt and betrayal.** The nonoffending parent has lost the sense of internal and external security of his/her family. The dynamics have been dramatically changed. In cases of incest, the nonoffending parent may have lost his/her spouse, parenting partner, and the stability, although illusory, of the family system. An alliance with members of the extended family and friends may be jeopardized. In extrafamilial abuse, friendships and neighborhoods can become battlegrounds.

9. **Sexual inadequacy or rejection.** In cases of incest, the nonoffending parent may feel as though the perpetrator turned to the child because the perpetrator was not sexually satisfied by the nonoffending parent.

10. **Financial fear.** If the perpetrator is the spouse, the nonoffending parent may become apprehensive regarding the family's financial security. As a result, he/she may resist the perpetrator's removal from the home and potential incarceration. Often, the abused child has siblings, and the nonoffending parent is concerned about all the children's financial welfare.

By being aware of the range of reactions of the nonoffending parent, the interviewer and team can better respond to him/her and the needs of the case. This does not imply that exhaustive therapy needs to be performed by these professionals; but an empathic and non-judgmental response will be of immense benefit to the nonoffending parent's ongoing therapy.

The team should keep the nonoffending parent as informed as possible. Information regarding the system and its operations, and child abuse materials (see Appendix D) can help the nonoffending parent to feel included in the process rather than just an observer. If the nonoffending parent is supportive, he/she should be informed of the potential course of the investigation and routinely informed of the status. Furthermore, the nonoffending parent should be told what is expected of him/her by the system. Few parents have been involved in a child abuse investigation, and guidance can significantly help them, thus, helping the investigative team.

The professionals involved do not need to alleviate the nonoffending parent's painful feelings, but rather acknowledge them. More beneficial is to immediately connect the nonoffending parent and child with services. As previously stated, this reduces the likelihood of recantation, but it also expedites healing. Likewise, the nonoffending parent should be shown he/she has a support person on the investigative team. Whether this person is a caseworker, detective, or advocate, the nonoffending parent should have someone with whom he/she can talk, vent, and learn the status of the investigation/intervention.

Experience shows that a support person other than the investigating detective or caseworker is advantageous. These professionals are the investigating agents, and the boundaries often are skewed if they become a support mechanism for the parent. The demands of investigating the case and the numerous others with which they are charged may not allow them the time that would be required to do the job well.

The nonoffending parent can be a valuable source of information for the interviewer (see Appendix E). Experience has shown that having the nonoffending parent complete a Child Behavioral Inventory before the interview can provide the interviewer with behaviors that can be discussed, facilitating the child's disclosure. Detectives can use the information during interrogations and treatment providers can use it to facilitate treatment planning.

Additionally, routinely questioning the nonoffending parent on the following topics can yield beneficial results, not only for the investigation but also for the nonoffending parent's sense of being supported.

1. *How have the disclosure and investigation been for you?* Not only does this statement project empathy, it can also provide for the exchange of valuable information. Based on the nonoffending parent's response, the interviewer can learn more about the parent's reaction to the disclosure, his/her feelings toward the child and toward the alleged perpetrator, and his/her perspective on the professionals and the system's response.

2. *Knowing that hindsight is 20/20, do some behaviors and situations stand out in your mind?* This phrasing, instead of asking whether the child had previously disclosed, to which the parent had minimal or no response, helps to elicit a response. If the parent is able to provide details, further dialogue can determine whether he/she deliberately ignored the signs and/or disclosure or was in an oppressive situation in which he/she could not respond.

3. *How are things between you and (the alleged perpetrator)?* If the allegation is incest, this question can produce information about the nonoffending parent's relationship with the alleged perpetrator. This question can also elicit information regarding possible domination and violence in the home by the alleged perpetrator and whether the nonoffending parent can and will protect the child. This question can yield valuable information regarding communication patterns and decision making in the home.

4. *How are things going between you and your child?* Areas addressed by this question are the potential for negative feelings toward the child, a desire that the secret had remained as such and life had remained as it was; or the nonoffending parent's desire to support and protect the child.

5. *Whom do you have for support? What do you need now?* This important question conveys concern for him/her and the present situation. Individuals who feel supported are more likely to share information and cooperate than are those who feel exploited. Also, in order to provide his/her child(ren) with the necessary support and protection, the nonoffending parent needs to feel supported.

6. *Are there any other areas in which your family could use assistance?* It is important to address the family as a whole rather than just focus on the abuse. Everyday issues and concerns continue in addition to the stress of the disclosure and subsequent investigation. Furthermore, in incest situations, it is more likely for the nonoffending parent to resist the alleged perpetrator's removal or have the perpetrator return soon after his/her removal if the basic needs, such as food and shelter, are not being fulfilled. Thus, because protection is pivotal, assistance is vital.

It is recommended that the interviewer complete a family needs assessment with the nonoffending parent at the time of the initial interview (see Appendix E).

7. If applicable, *What are your greatest concerns regarding your spouse's removal from the home (now and in the future)?* It is important to assess where his/her greatest concerns lie for the reasons previously stated.

8. *What do you know about child abuse (someone you have known, a television talk show, etc.)?* It places a nonoffending parent in an arduous situation to be directly asked if he/she was victimized as a child. This is a highly charged topic to discuss with a professional one has known for only five minutes, and under precarious circumstances. Yet, it is unwise to avoid the topic altogether. Thus, asking in this manner can yield useful information.

9. *How would you like to see the future for you, your child(ren), and the alleged perpetrator?* This helps show the interviewer the nonoffending parent's stance on reunification, prosecution, and motivation for treatment.

In cases involving an extended forensic assessment, additional information can be obtained. The nonoffending parent has a lengthier assessment during which more detailed information can be gathered. This information is beneficial not only to the evaluation process, but also the therapeutic process.

A component of the discussion with the nonoffending parent is a referral for mental health services. The parent needs to understand that although the child may appear "fine" or the parent may want to "put the abuse behind" them, feelings regarding the abuse and the effects of abuse can hide within the child. The professional should explain that if these are not dealt with professionally, they eventually may become problems. The professional should explain the long-term, devastating effects of abuse. Furthermore, he/she should explain the role and benefits of treatment, and recommend competent professionals.

In all child sexual abuse interviews, it is important to start the dialogue with what is most important for the individual being interviewed. This often means all the questions for the nonoffending parent may not be addressed during the initial visit. This is fine. What is most important is for the nonoffending parent to feel supported and receive systemic information, and for the professional to determine whether the child will be protected from further harm. All other areas can be addressed in subsequent interviews.

REFERENCES:

Cammaert, L. (1988). Non-offending mothers: A new conceptualization. In L.E.A. Walker (Ed.), *Handbook on sexual abuse of children* (pp. 309-325). New York: Springer Publishing Co.

Groth, N. (1979). *Men who rape: The psychology of the offender.* New York: Plenum Press.

Ovaris, W. (1995). *After the nightmare: The treatment of non-offending mothers of sexually abused children.* Holmes Beach, FL: Learning Publications.

Sgroi, S., & Dana, N. (1982). Individual and group treatment of mothers of incest victims. In S. Sgroi (Ed.), *Handbook of Clinical Intervention in Child Sexual Abuse.* Lexington, MA: Lexington Books.

Chapter 16

FORMING CONCLUSIONS

Following the interview or extended forensic assessment and the acommpanying investigation, all that has been disclosed and gathered needs to be analyzed. As has been stressed throughout this book, the child's disclosure is just one component of the investigative process. Deciding whether there is a valid allegation of child abuse should not be based exclusively on the data provided from the child's interview/assessment. Likewise, a case should not be terminated based on the absence of a disclosure. All sources should be appraised and evaluated.

Once the team has completed the comprehensive investigation, the case should be stringently reviewed. Carnes and Steinmetz (1996) developed a disclosure credibility desk guide to facilitate this review. The guide is not an empirically normed and tested scale, scores are not given and used to determine the validity of abuse. It is a desk guide, designed to assist the team in analyzing the results of the investigation/assessment. It helps review the case systematically. The elements of the guide are drawn from research on statement validity analysis. The team checks appliciable items.

NCAC CREDIBILTY DESK GUIDE

The presence or absence of any given element does not validate or invalidate a child's statement; rather, the elements are provided as a framework for analyzing the investigation/assessment outcome.

1. _____ Child made verbal disclosure.

2. _____ Child provided a demonstration of abuse.

_____ Dolls

_____ Anatomical drawings

_____ Free-style drawings

_____ Other_____

3. _____ Child provided a description of abuse to someone else.

_____ Another professional

_____ A family member or friend

_____ Other _____

4. _____ Child provided the majority of details from a first-person perspective.

5. _____ Child demonstrated freedom to correct the interviewer.

6. _____ Child demonstrated freedom to say, "I don't know; I don't remember; I don't understand; I don't want to talk about it."

7. _____ Disclosure was somewhat unstructured without rote quality.

8. Specific details recounted:

_____ Alleged perpetrator clearly identified.

_____ Specific chargeable offense identified.

_____ Date identified within two-month time frame.

_____ Time of day identified.

_____ Place(s) of alleged offense(s) identified.

_____ Sensory details provided.

_____ Unique and idiosyncratic details provided.

_____ Peripheral details (decorations, furnishings) provided.

_____ Props (lotions, pornography, photography, gadgets) described.

_____ Grooming behavior identified.

_____ Use of force or threats described.

_____ Maintenance of secret (force, threats, coercion) described.

_____ Presence of others described.

_____ Possibility of different perpetrator ruled out.

_____ Specifics of own clothing described.

_____ Specifics of alleged perpetrator's clothing described.

_____ Pattern of abuse plausible.

_____ Core factors identified consistently.

_____ Verbatim quote of an utterance made by another person present during the alleged incident provided.

_____ "Unexpected complication" that caused an interruption of the alleged incident (i.e. "The doorbell rang and he had to stop.") recounted.

_____ Alleged perpetrator's mental or emotional state (i.e., "it was like he was mad and his face was scrunched up.") described.

_____ Another person's presence in the building or general area during the alleged incident, who did not witness the event, described.

_____ Justification of alleged perpetrator's actions attempted.

9. _____ Disclosure is consistent with developmental level.

_____ Sexual knowledge and/or terminology is beyond the typical developmental level for a child this age.

_____ General terminology describing the alleged offense is developmentally appropriate.

_____ Child verbalized understanding of truth versus lie.

_____ Child verbalized understanding and accepted obligation to tell the truth.

_____ Child verbalized understanding of the consequences of telling a lie.

_____ Details of time are age appropriate.

_____ Details of location are age appropriate.

_____ Detail of acts described are age appropriate.

_____ Identification of the alleged perpetrator is age appropriate.

_____ Cognitive/developmental abilities are age appropriate and support allegation validity.

10. Emotional content (in relation to the child's known coping style)

_____ Child appeared hesitant to disclose.

Manifestation_____

_____ Child appeared withdrawn.

Manifestation_____

_____ Child appeared guarded.

Manifestation_____

_____ Child exhibited embarrassment during disclosure.

Manifestation_____

_____ Child exhibited guilt during disclosure.

Manifestation_____

_____ Child exhibited anxiety during disclosure.

Manifestation_____

_____ Child exhibited disgust during disclosure.

Manifestation_____

_____ Child exhibited anger during disclosure.

Manifestation_____

_____ Child exhibited sexual arousal during disclosure.

Manifestation_____

_____ Child exhibited fear during disclosure.

Manifestation_____

_____ Child's affect was flat.

_____ Child's affect was congruent with the disclosure.

If not, describe the incongruence. _____

_____

11. Behavioral checklist results.

_____ Inappropriate sexual behaviors shown on the Friedrich Child Sexual Behavior Index.

_____ Child has borderline or clinical scores on the Achenbach Child Behavior Checklist.

_____ Child has significant behaviors on Child Behavioral Inventory.

12. Collaborative information/confirmatory factors

_____ Law enforcement has crime scene evidence.

_____ Alleged perpetrator has confessed.

_____ Alleged perpetrator has failed the polygraph examination.

_____ Medical findings indicate the possibility of abuse.

_____ Eyewitness corroboration has been obtained.

_____ Behavioral or situational witness has been obtained.

_____ Behavioral or situational confirmatory factors exist.

_____ Other victims of the alleged perpetrator have disclosed.

_____ Alleged perpetrator has been previously investigated by law enforcement or child protective services.

_____ Alleged perpetrator has been convicted of child sexual abuse and/or other sexual crimes previously.

13. Motivational factors

_____ Interviewer explored for possible secondary gain.

_____ Interviewer explored for evidence the child was coached to disclose.

_____ Interviewer explored for evidence the child was pressured not to disclose.

_____ Interviewer explored child's explanation of timing of present disclosure.

Comments on motivational factors: _____

_____

_____

14. Alternative explanations

_____ Interviewer explored for possibility of specific psychiatric disorder that impairs perceptions of reality.

_____ Interviewer explored for possibility that a benign activity (i.e., bathing) was misinterpreted.

_____ Interviewer explored for possibility of third-party coaching.

_____ Interviewer explored for possibility of other dysfunction in the child's life.

_____ Interviewer explored nature of any improbable or unusual elements.

_____ Other _____

Comments on alternative explanations: _____

_____

_____

Based on the above analysis, the most likely hypothesis is:

_____ The child has made a valid report of abuse.

_____ The child disclosed abuse. The disclosure is vague or problematic due to developmental and/or cognitive limitations of the child.

_____ The child disclosed abuse. The fundamental allegation appears to be valid, based on the above criteria. However, improbable or unusual elements are incorporated into various details, leaving some aspects of the disclosure to be invalidated based on the above criteria.

_____ The child disclosed abuse. The fundamental allegation may be valid, but it appears that efforts to coach or shape the child have led to additional allegations that cannot be validated based on the above criteria.

_____ Child did not disclose abuse. Behavioral or other indicators exist that are consistent with those present in abused children.

_____ The child appears to have been coached, pressured, or shaped to make a disclosure that cannot be validated by the above criteria.

_____ Child appears to be utilizing past victimization as a basis for present disclosure.

_____ The child appears to have made a disclosure that is based on personal motives of revenge, secondary gain, or attempts to help someone.

_____ Due to the psychiatric disturbance in the child, the disclosure cannot be validated by the above criteria.

_____ Due to developmental and/or cognitive limitations of the child, the disclosure cannot be validated by the above criteria.

_____ Other _____

_____

When the guide is completed, the team is ready to make many decisions. Based on the evidence, does the allegation appear to be valid? If the allegation appears dubious, what are the most effective interventions to resolve the situation? If the allegations appear to be valid, is there enough evidence for prosecution or should the emphasis of the case be civil/protection?

If the team is still unsure of the credibility of the allegation, what should be the next step? Whose rights have precedence? What level of dysfunction is a parent allowed? How can the team best intervene in a secondary or tertiary preventative manner?

What are the most effective interventions for the child and the family? Is it safe to return this child to his/her home? If so, will the child be supported and protected from further harm? Are other children in the home? Are they also protected? Will the alleged perpetrator remain out of the home? Is there a need for a short-term/shelter placement? Is there a possibility of placement with a relative? Can services be mandated for nonoffending family members?

There are no "correct" answers for these questions. Rather, some of the same principles incorporated into investigative interviewing apply: Be objective; minimize the harm; balance the forensic with the therapeutic; and remember that no standard response exists.

Recall that it is the truth that is being sought, not the substantiation of the allegation.

If information or evidence is missing, the team must exhaust every resource to find it or accept that it is not obtainable. The team must consider and explore every alternative explanation for the allegation. For as harmful as it is for a child to be returned to a perpetrating environment, it is equally injurious to falsely accuse an innocent person.

Now that Pandora's box has been opened, it is wise to promptly connect the child and family with services. However, the team should look carefully at all the family is being asked to do. If expectations are insurmountable, issues should be prioritized.

Finally, another aspect of balancing is to recall the symmetry between the forensic and the therapeutic. Prosecution is but one of the focal points. Prevention and intervention also must be addressed. Therapeutic interventions need to be provided, regardless of the forensic status of the case. Treatment is not only to resolve the effects of the victimization, but to prevent dysfunctional outcomes and exploitive behaviors. However, the intervention course varies. As has been reiterated throughout the book, there is no set response to abuse. Thus, there should not be a rubber stamp set response to each case. Rather, each individual/family should be assessed for individualized needs.

REFERENCES:

Carnes, C., & Steinmetz, M. (1996). *National Children's Advocacy Center Disclosure Reliability Desk Guide.*

Child's Name _____ Case # _____

EXTENDED FORENSIC ASSESSMENT NONOFFENDING PARENT INTERVIEW

1. Child Sexual Behavioral Inventory   Date completed_____

2. Clinical interview

      Information obtained from_____

      Relationship to child_____

      Information obtained by_____

DATE A. Present concerns (child, siblings, self, family, system)

      B. Having completed CSBI, what items/behaviors are prominent/of concern?

      C. Behaviors noticed in child (and description)

          1. Affective

              a. Cries a lot

DATE

b. Feels worthless/inferior

c. Fears certain places, things, and people

d. Unresponsive to affection

e. Easily gives affection

f. Shy/timid

g. Stubborn, sullen, or irritable

h. Sudden changes in mood or feelings

i. Withdrawn

j. Unusual amount of worries, difficulty relaxing

k. Emotionally numb

l. Holds anger inside

2. Peer relations

a. Prefers same-age playmates

b. Prefers older playmates

DATE   c. Prefers younger playmates

                        d. Develops harmful or unhealthy relationships

                        e. Shy/uneasy around opposite gender

        3. Cognitive

                        a. Has difficulty concentrating/paying attention

                        b. Feels he/she has to be perfect

                        c. Hears voices no one else hears

                        d. Appears preoccupied

                        e. Talks about not liking his/her own gender

        4. Physical

                        a. Somatic complaints of stomachaches, headaches, and/or pains

                        b. Change in appetite

DATE   c. Talks about not liking his/her body

   5. Self-destructive

      a. Deliberately harms self

      b. Talks about killing self/being dead

      c. Attempts suicide

   6. Behavioral

      a. Lost interest in things he/she once enjoyed

      b. Refuses to talk and/or is secretive

      c. Runs away from home

      d. Defiant

      e. Sets fires

      f. Problems at school (truancy/grades)

      g. Threatens people

      h. Minor criminal violations

      i. Major criminal violations

DATE

j. Alcohol/drug use

k. Can't sit still/restless

l. Cruel to animals

m. Doesn't like to be touched

n. Destroys property (own/others)

o. Physically attacks others

p. Smears/plays with feces/urine

q. Strange behaviors

D. Prenatal and early childhood history

    1. Conception (planned/unplanned, your reaction, "spouse" reaction)

    2. Pregnancy (perception, medical issues)

    3. Delivery (complications, perception, medical problems)

DATE 4. Major life events (loss/separations: child and family members)

5. Developmental milestones (walking, talking, toilet training, etc.)

E. Family information

1. Present composition of home

2. Changes in composition (who, when, and why)

3. If divorce is pending, obtain information on dispute of custody, visitation patterns, reason for divorce

4. History of domestic violence

5. History of substance abuse

6. History of psychiatric and medical problems

DATE F. Family patterns

    1. Communication/decision making

    2. Discipline (type used, who administers, child's response)

    3. Relationships (genogram)

    4. Sleeping configurations (how often does the child sleep with an adult, does the child share a room/bed; with whom; why; where does your child usually sleep)

    5. Child's sleep habits (bed-wetting, does the child have trouble falling asleep, nightmares, cries out in sleep, wakes up often at night, sleeps more/less than others)

DATE   6. Bathing (does child bathe alone; if no, with whom; does child ask or need help with bathing; who assists)

G. Sexual mores

   1. Are there pictures of nude people available in your child's home now?

   2. Have there been pictures of nude people in previous homes of your child?

   3. Is there cable television in the child's home? (what type of channels)

   4. Has your child seen sexual activities? If so, what (on T.V., in movie, and/or in real life)?

   5. Has your child overheard discussions/arguments/details of your sexual activities?

DATE   6. How do you think children should learn about sex and sexuality?

       7. Attitudes toward masturbation (is it okay, when is it all right, by whom, under what circumstances)

       8. Attitudes toward nudity

H. Sexual, physical, and emotional abuse history

       1. Nonoffending parent

       2. Alleged perpetrator

       3. Siblings

DATE   4. Identified child

I. Present allegation

    1. How did you learn of the alleged abuse?

    2. Your initial reaction/response

    3. Child's disclosure (in parent's words, cross-reference with child's story)

    4. Family member's reactions to child's disclosure and ensuing events

    5. Motivation for recovery/change (nonoffending parent, perpetrator, child, siblings)

DATE J. Support system

K. How are you feeling now, after today's interview?

L. What are your future concerns for yourself, child, his/her siblings, and, if applicable, the alleged perpetrator?

CHILD BEHAVIORAL INVENTORY

Child's Name _____ Case # _____

DATE:_____

INFORMATION PROVIDED BY:_____

Listed below are behaviors some children may exhibit. Some behaviors might occur only in certain age groups. If a behavior occurs sometimes, often or very often, please write on the line (if you can) the approximate date you first noticed the behavior. There is a place on the bottom where you can share additional information. Please know any information you share will be helpful.

	NEVER	RARELY	SOMETIMES	OFTEN	VERY OFTEN	N/A
ANXIETY Suddenly gets panic or anxiety attacks						
Has a hard time relaxing						
Easily startled						
Overly active						
Lacks concentration/has difficulty remembering						
Inability to recall specific events						
Gets confused easily						

COMMENTS:

	NEVER	RARELY	SOMETIMES	OFTEN	VERY OFTEN	N/A
Has an imaginary companion						
Hears voices that no one else hears						
See things no one else can						
Difficulty making decisions						
Unable to stop thinking about or going over certain events						
"Spaces out" or has out-of-body experience						
Makes up or exaggerates events or statements						
Daydreams, appears preoccupied						
Unusual number of worries						
PHYSICAL Trouble staying asleep						
Nightmares						
Dreams about sexual abuse						

COMMENTS:

	NEVER	RARELY	SOMETIMES	OFTEN	VERY OFTEN	N/A
Problems with substance abuse						
Complains of stomach-aches, headaches, pains						
Continual and un-explained vomiting						
Change in appetite						
Takes unnecessary risks, puts self in danger						
Develops harmful or unhealthy relationships						
AVOIDANCE Difficulty making/ keeping friends						
Shy or uneasy with opposite gender						
Difficulty getting along with other family members						
Avoids abuse-related thoughts and feelings						
Fearful of certain places, things, people						
Loses interest in doing things he/she used to enjoy						

COMMENTS:

	NEVER	RARELY	SOMETIMES	OFTEN	VERY OFTEN	N/A
BEHAVIORAL Friends significantly older or younger						
Acts younger than age						
Sexually absorbed in talk and play						
Sexually improper behavior (masturbates in public, touches others)						
Unusual interest in or specific knowledge of sexual acts						
Practices unprotected sex						
Prostitutes self						
Sexually harms others						
Community conflict (e.g., destroying others' property)						
Overly pushy (e.g., hitting)						
Defiant/rebellious						
Gets mad easily						
Irritable						
Problems at school (e.g., grades)						

COMMENTS:

	NEVER	RARELY	SOMETIMES	OFTEN	VERY OFTEN	N/A
Problems at school (e.g., truancy)						
Makes statements about being sexually abused						
Body mutilation (cutting self)						
Minor criminal violations (e.g., shoplifting)						
Doesn't like to be touched						
Uncontrollable behavior (e.g., excessive handwashing)						
Runs away						
Wears many layers of clothing						
Reluctant to go home after school						
Secretive behavior						
Indirect hints						
Easily gives affection to people he/she does not know						
Serious criminal problems (assault)						
Doesn't finish things						

COMMENTS

	NEVER	RARELY	SOMETIMES	OFTEN	VERY OFTEN	N/A
EMOTIONAL Gets scared around specific gender						
Fearful to leave home						
Reluctant to go to certain places or with certain people						
Unwilling to dress for or participate in gym class						
Hates or fears sex or the idea of sex						
Emotionally numb						
Holds anger inside						
Has difficulty trusting						
Sense of overwhelming responsibilty						
Expresses feelings of no future						
Overly agreeable, extremely obedient						
Depressed, sad, or withdrawn						
Sleeps more than usual						
Drastic mood swings						
Tries too hard to please						

COMMENTS:

	NEVER	RARELY	SOMETIMES	OFTEN	VERY OFTEN	N/A
Emotional (cries easily), very sensitive						
Has guilty feelings						
Blames self						
Doesn't like body						
Feels inferior						
Low self-esteem						
Hurts self physically						
Thinks or talks about suicide						
Attempts suicide						

COMMENTS:

EXTENDED FORENSIC ASSESSMENT REPORT OUTLINE

1. Identifying information
    A. Name
    B. Date of birth
    C. Dates of sessions
    D. Where sessions were conducted and by whom
    E. Length of sessions
    F. Collateral sources reviewed

2. Presenting problem
    A. Referral source
    B. Reason for initial referral
    C. If and when interviewed, by whom, where
    D. Who was present at the investigation interview
    E. Result of interview (if disclosure, what; the course of intervention; why EFA requested)
    F. If abuse is disclosed during EFA, gather the following information (items should be addressed for each alleged perpetrator)
        1. Type of abuse
            a. Acts leading up to the alleged abuse
            b. Acts in the alleged abuse
            c. Instruments and/or pornography
        2. Characteristics of the abuse situation
            a. Duration
            b. Frequency
            c. Use of force
            d. Threats about disclosure
            e. Presence of others
        3. Reaction to abuse and perpetrator
        4. Disclosure efforts
    G. Disclosure elements
        1. Is explicit detail given?
        2. Is the disclosure rote (first-person delivery)?
        3. Are there unique and distinguishing factors about the alleged perpetrator and the alleged abuse?
        4. Is the disclosure age appropriate?
        5. Is there a pattern of abuse?
        6. Is there motive for disclosure?
        7. Consistency of disclosure/coherence and redundancy versus confabulation
    H. Reaction/consequences of the alleged abuse
        1. If age appropriate, the child's view
        2. Behavioral (take developmental factors into consideration)

 a. Sexual behavior exhibited/reported
    1. Acting out on others
       a. Classification
       b. Explanation
          1. Age difference
          2. Size difference
          3. Status difference
          4. Type of activity
          5. Personality of activity
          6. Child's sexual development
    2. Exhibited behaviors
       a. Excessive masturbation
       b. Public masturbation, after reprimand
       c. Frequently asks to be touched or touches adults genitals/chest
       d. Simulated intercourse on inanimate objects, adult's legs, animals, etc.
       e. Excessive sexual play with dolls/toys
       f. Preoccupation with discussing "sex"
       g. Sexually graphic drawings
       h. Anger, aggressiveness, and/or sadness about sex roles, own or other gender, or own genitals
       i. Promiscuity
       j. Inappropriate sexual knowledge
       k. Other
 b. Nonsexual behaviors
    1. Regressive tendencies
    2. School-related difficulties
    3. Aggression/delinquency
    4. Self-mutilative behaviors
    5. Eating disorders
    6. Sleeping disturbances
    7. Fears/anxieties
    8. Substance abuse
    9. Self-esteem and social skills obstacles
    10. Running away
    11. Fire setting
D. Family
  1. Prenatal and early childhood history
  2. Family information
    a. Composition
    b. Divorce/custody

   c. Communication patterns
   d. Discipline patterns
   e. Relationships
   f. History of abuse
  3. History of domestic violence
  4. History of substance abuse
  5. History of psychological/need problems
  6. Present allegations
   a. Reaction
   b. Response
  7. Support structure
 E. Collaborative reports
  1. Law enforcement
  2. Child protective services
  3. Medical examination
  4. Social services
  5. Treatment providers
  6. Foster parents
  7. School/day care
  8. Polygraph
  9. Child Behavioral Inventory
  10. Nonoffending parent interview
  11. Extended family member reports

4. Treatment recommendations
 A. Child
  1. State determination and explain (use analysis process detailed in NCAC Desk Guide)
  2. Child protective issues
   a. Risk of harm
   b. Need for alternative placement
  3. A child sexual abuse specific referral and recommendations for mental health services
 B. Other family members – Abuse specific referral and recommendations for enhancement of child's recovery and own areas of resolution

The following pages are a copy of a pamphlet used at the Elkhart County (Indiana) Child and Family Advocacy Center. Although most of the information is applicable in all states, some information is specific to Indiana.

WALKING

THROUGH

THE

SYSTEM

A Step - by -Step Guide
If You Suspect Your Child
Has Been Abused

Introduction

If you suspect or have become aware that your child has been abused (emotionally, physically, and/or sexually) this booklet is for you. It contains information on the system of agencies with whom you'll come in contact. Hopefully, by knowing what to expect from these agencies, your anxiety will be lessened, your cooperation with the various agencies will be more productive, and additional frustrations will be decreased.

Family members often feel very alone and drawn apart during and after such crisis. It is important for you to know that there is a system of agencies available to you to provide guidance and support. Please do not hesitate to ask questions and for assistance.

Reporting suspected child abuse is the first step toward yours and your child's recovery.

Learning Your Child May Have Been Abused

The most common initial reaction to a child's disclosure of abuse is denial. As parents, you do not want to believe your child has been harmed. Unfortunately, if you do not listen to your child and report the abuse, your child will continue to be at risk of further abuse, and will not fully recover without the assistance of outside help.

Learning that your child may have been abused can be very confusing and frightening to not only your child, but you. Some helpful tips to use with your child are:

1. Quietly encourage your child to tell you about the abuse.

2. Try not to overreact – your child needs support, not to feel like they made you mad or sad.

3. Let your child know it was not their fault that they were abused.

4. Let your child know how glad you are that they had the courage to tell.

5. Thank your child for sharing this information.

6. Let your child know you will help them and protect them from the abuse happening again.

7. Let your child know they are not in trouble.

What Is Going To Happen?
(From Investigation Through Prosecution)

Every report of child abuse is individual and unique, however listed below are the steps that are often followed.

REPORTING:
It is mandatory (Indiana State law) that all suspicions of child abuse and neglect be reported immediately.

1. A report is made, usually by phone, to the local child protective services or law enforcement agency.

2. After the report is made, a law enforcement officer and child protective services worker will become a team to investigate the report.

INITIAL RESPONSE:

1. Within 24 hours, the team will meet briefly with you and/or your child to check out the details of the report and determine if there is reason to believe the abuse took place.

2. If there are indications that your child has been abused, the team will arrange a time with you to interview your child in a more formal manner.

PROTECTIVE CUSTODY:

1. The safety of your child is the primary concern. If the offender is living in the home, he or she will be asked to leave the home. If the offender refuses to leave, the non-offending parent will be asked to leave the home with the child. If neither of these arrangements is possible, or the non-offending parent is unable to protect the child, the child will be temporarily placed in protective custody and placed in a foster home, shelter or relative's home.

2. If your child is taken into protective custody, there will be a detention hearing in Juvenile Court. This hearing must occur within 72 hours (excluding weekends and holidays) of the time your child was detained. At this hearing, the child protective services worker will be present. The worker must justify to the Court why the child was taken into protective custody, the Court must decide whether to continue placement or return the child home.

THE INTERVIEWS:

1. This interview will usually last about 1 hour. This time includes your child's interview and your interview. Your child will separate from you and meet with a professional in a specially decorated room for children. This interview will last no longer than 45 minutes. After this interview, you will be separated from your child and will be asked to share what you know about the report, your child's behavior changes, and other important information about the abuse allegation. This is a good time for you to ask the team questions. You are probably curious about what will happen next. Don't be discouraged if their answers are vague. They are still reviewing your child's statement and the information you shared with them.

2. When scheduling this interview, please let the scheduling person know what times of the day are best for your child. Please keep in mind his or her naps, mealtimes, school, etc.

3. If your child has particular fears (of women, of men, anything), please tell the scheduling person.

4. It is very important that you do not questioin your child at length before the interview takes place. Don't keep going over the facts with your child unless he or she brings it up. But don't pretend it didn't happen either.

5. Before leaving the Child and Family Advocacy Center, make sure you write down everyone's name and number, so you'll know whom to contact in the future if you have questions.

6. Please do not question your child about the interview. They probably have many feelings about it, allow them to talk about their feelings if they bring them up.

MEDICAL EXAMINATION:

A medical examination (with the doctor or at the hospital) may occur to determine if your child has been physically harmed and to check on your child's well-being. The doctors work cooperatively with the team and they will share the findings with each other so your child does not have to be re-interviewed. If your child has been harmed, the doctor will let you know and treat your child.

PROSECUTION:

After the interview, medical examination, and the collection of other information, the law enforcement officer involved will decide if the information obtained should be referred to the prosecuting attorney's office. The prosecutor will decide if the case should go through the criminal court system.

1. If the prosecutor does not file a charge, you have the right to find out the reason. (Please know that child abuse cases can be very difficult to prove, and the prosecutor does not want to subject you and your child to the court process if it does not look like it will be beneficial to your child.)

2. If the prosecutor files charges, a warrant for the arrest of the alleged offender will be issued.

3. After the arrest, the alleged offender will appear in front of a Judge, and if probable cause is found, the Judge will set bond and schedule a date for the arraignment hearing.

ARRAIGNMENT HEARING:

The arraignment is when the alleged offender appears before the Judge and is advised of his/her rights. The Judge will enter a not guilty plea for the defendant, and the court will set future hearing dates.

BEFORE THE TRIAL:

Every case is different, so not every case will go through the same steps. The following is a listing of the possibilities that may occur:

Pre-trial Hearings: This is a hearing where the evidence is reviewed. You may be asked to be present. If you are required to attend, you will receive a subpoena. This is a document from the court and it will tell you when and where to appear.

Plea-Bargaining: Plea bargaining may take place between the prosecuting attorney and the defense attorney at any time after the pre-trial hearing. They negotiate a plea of guilty, for the offender, often reducing the original charge. This could mean there would be no trial, no chance of acquittal, and a lesser sentence.

Depositions: A deposition is when you and/or your child will meet with the prosecuting attorney and the defense attorney to share your account of the incidents.

COURT PREPARATION:

A court appearance can be temporarily frightening or overwhelming for your child but, with some preparation, there should not be any long term, negative effects.

To assist your child, and better prepare them for what may occur at the trial, some type of preparation will occur. Court preparation can include: visiting a courtroom, meeting with the advocate to discuss feelings and information, courtroom activity books to be completed at home or in counseling, and a meeting with the Prosecutor. (For more information on this, contact Victim Assistance or the Child and Family Advocacy Center.)

INFORMATION:

It may seem as though things are moving so slowly, and this may be frustrating to you and your family. However, things must be completed in certain ways and in specific order. The professionals involved do care and are doing their jobs very carefully. If they do not do a thorough job, they may not be able to gather all the necessary facts and evidence. It is alright for you to contact Victim Assistance to inquire about the status of your case and to find out other relevant information.

The Trial – There are two types of trials, a bench trial (at which there is no jury), or a jury trial (at which the judge and a jury of 12 people are present). However, most cases do not go to trial.

During the trial, you, your child, and other witnesses will be asked to testify. In addition, the results of the medical examination, and the team investigation will be presented. The prosecuting attorney will begin the questioning and then the defense attorney will question you and may try to dispute what you say. If the defendant is found guilty, he/she has a right to appeal. A not guilty finding cannot be appealed by the prosecuting attorney.

Please remember, whatever the verdict is, know that you made the right decision to report the abuse and that a not guilty verdict does not mean that the abuse was not committed.

Sentencing – the sentence is determined by the Judge. You will be invited to submit a written statement, which he/she will review.

Emotional Recovery

COUNSELING: Many people prefer to think that they can care for their own worries and troubles, but when your child has been abused, the stress of the experience (disclosure and investigation), and the long term negative effects of the abuse, really need to be discussed with a trained professional. Your child, your other family members, and yourself should find counseling helpful. Your caseworker or the Child and Family Advocacy Center can provide you with names of agencies who provide counseling, classes and related services that will assist you.

VICTIM ASSISTANCE: This program may be helpful to you. Victim Assistance is a resource, support and liaison agency. It can assist you with court information, violent and sex crime compensation, court preparation and connection with community services.

CASA: A CASA (court appointed special advocate) is a volunteer who is interested in you and your child. The Judge asks a CASA to be available to see and listen to your child regularly. The CASA's job is to learn about your child and your family and tell the Judge what they think would be best. The CASA can also tell the Judge what your child wants to have happen. The CASA is primarily used in Juvenile Court.

DIVISION OF FAMILY AND CHILDREN'S SERVICES:
CASEWORKERS: The caseworkers' role is to assist families who have children who may have been victims of child abuse or neglect. Services are offered through referral to community medical and social service agencies.

HOME-BASED INTENSIVE WORKER: This worker assists your caseworker. The home-based service worker will meet with you and your family on a more frequent basis than your caseworker. This worker can also assist you with transportation, job searches, locating appropriate services, and acting as an objective sounding board to you. Not every case has this type of caseworker.

Juvenile Court Process

It is important that you attend every Court Hearing concerning you and your child. You may receive notice of a hearing by legal notice in the mail, in person or by a telephone call. Below is a listing of the different hearings:

1. *Detention Hearing.* (Discussed on page 165)

2. *Initial Hearing* – The Court tells you and your child about the information the team has brought to the court; and the Court asks you to admit or deny the charges.

3. *Fact-finding Hearing* – The Judge hears evidence from everyone and makes a decision whether your child is abused and/or neglected.

4. *Disposition Hearing* – If your child is found by the Judge to be abused and/or neglected, the Judge will consider all the recommendations concerning your child, including your recommendations. A decision will then be made by the Judge as to the plan for your child's future.

5. *Parental Participation Hearing* – Your involvement in services to help yourself or your child are addressed at this hearing.

6. *Review Hearings* – are held every twelve months and every eighteen months, after the date of the removal of your child from your home or after the date of the Disposition

hearing. The Judge listens to everyone's reports on the case and then decides whether to continue with the original plan or make changes.

7. *Contempt Hearings* – If you fail to follow a Court Order, the Court can hold a hearing to determine if you are in Contempt of Court for failure to follow the Court Order. There are various consequences if you are found to be in Contempt of Court.

8. *Delinquent Proceedings* – If the alleged perpetrator is a juvenile, proceedings will take place in Juvenile Court.

PARENT INTAKE FORM

DATE:_____

NAME OF CHILD: _____ BIRTHDATE: _____

CHILD'S SCHOOL: _____

PARENT(S) NAME (identify relationship, i.e., natural/step):

_____

_____

SIBLING(S) NAME (identify relationship, i.e., half, step, natural):

_____

_____

ADDRESS:_____ZIP: _____

TELEPHONE:_____

1. What is the best time of the day for you and your child to attend future appointments?

(We do not want to interrupt nap time, special activities, etc.)

_____

2. Is your child seeing a therapist? If so, what are the therapist's name and address?

_____

_____

3. When was the last time your child had contact with the alleged perpetrator?

_____

4. Is your child taking any medications? If yes, please list:

_____

_____

THANK YOU FOR YOUR TIME AND WILLINGNESS TO COMPLETE THIS FORM.

_____   _____
            Signature   Relationship to child

FAMILY NEEDS ASSESSMENT
(used in conjunction with EFA)

CLIENT'S NAME _____ DATE _____

CASEWORKER'S NAME _____

Instructions: Circle applicable items.

1. Emotional stability
   a. No evidence of emotional instability or psychiatric disorders
   b. One caregiver has moderate problems that interfere with functioning
   c. One caregiver has problems that severely limit functioning
   d. Both caregivers/parents have moderate to severe problems

2. Parenting skills
   a. Caregivers have appropriate skills; there are no known deficits
   b. One caregiver needs improvement
   c. Both caregivers need improvement
   d. Either caregiver repeatedly displays abusive, neglectful, and/or destructive parenting patterns

3. Substance abuse
   a. No evidence of abuse
   b. One caretaker has history of abuse
   c. Both caretakers have history of abuse
   d. Caretaker(s)is (are) in treatment

4. Domestic relations
   a. Supportive relationship/no evidence of threatening or assaultive behavior toward family members
   b. Marital discord/lack of cooperation/isolated incidents of violent behavior, no injury resulted
   c. Serious marital discord/current patterns of intimidation, threats of harm, and violence; any incident resulting in injury

5. Support system
   a. Family has available, and uses, external support system
   b. Family has limited support system
   c. No support system available
   d. Family needs support system but is reluctant to use one
   e. Family has a dysfunctional support system

6. Child(ren) characteristics/problems
   a. Child(ren) has (have) no known emotional, behavioral, intellectual, or physical problems
   b. Child(ren) has (have) minor problems, but little impact on functioning
   c. Child(ren) have problems in one or more areas that sometimes limit functioning
   d. One child has severe/chronic problems that result in serious dysfunction
   e. Two or more children have severe/chronic problems that result in serious dysfunction

7. Environmental
   a. Family has adequate housing, clothing, and nutrition
   b. Physical environment presents potential hazards to family members' health/safety
   c. Conditions exist in household that have caused illness/injury
   d. Family has been evicted/homeless

8. Financial
   a. Family income is sufficient to meet needs and is adequately managed/employment is secured or not needed
   b. Income limited but adequately managed/unemployed but looking
   c. Income insufficient or not well-managed; unable to meet basic needs/responsibilities
   d. Family is in financial crisis/unemployed and not interested in securing

9. Health
   a. Caregiver(s) has (have) no known health problems that affect functioning
   b. Caregiver(s) has (have) moderate disability/illness; impairs ability to care for child(ren)
   c. Serious disability/illness; severely limits ability to care for child(ren)

10. Intellectual ability
   a. No evidence of limitation in caregiver's intellectual functioning/ caretaker has at least basic education skills and functional literacy skills
   b. Caregiver has somewhat limited intellectual functioning/ caregiver marginally educated or literate, creates some problems
   c. Caregiver's intellectual ability severely limits ability to function, or illiterate

11. Abuse/neglect history
    a. Neither caregiver has a history of abuse/neglect
    b. Either caregiver is a victim of abuse/neglect and has not received treatment
    c. Either caregiver is a victim of abuse/neglect and has received treatment
    d. Either caregiver is an alleged perpetrator but is receptive/receiving and completed treatment
    e. Either caregiver is an alleged perpetrator and is resistant or has not received treatment

12. Delinquent behaviors
    a. Child has no known delinquent behaviors
    b. Child has a few delinquent behaviors (status offense)
    c. Child has a few delinquent behaviors that have or are requiring intervention
    d. Child has several delinquent behaviors that have or are requiring intervention

13.School behaviors
    a. Child has no known school behavioral problems
    b. Child has a few known school behavioral problems
    c. Child has numerous known school behavioral problems resulting in suspension or expulsion